THE PICTORIAL
ENCYCLOPEDIA OF

HORSES

THE PICTORIAL ENCYCLOPEDIA OF
HORSES

WJ YENNE

GALLERY BOOKS
An imprint of W.H. Smith Publishers Inc.
112 Madison Avenue
New York, New York 10016

Published by Gallery Books
A Division of WH Smith Publishers Inc
112 Madison Avenue
New York, NY 10016

Produced by
Brompton Books Corp
15 Sherwood Place
Greenwich, CT 06830

ISBN 0-8317-6910-6
Printed in Spain by Printer Industria Gráfica, S.A.
Barcelona

10 9 8 7 6 5 4 3 2 1

Designed by Ruth DeJauregui
Edited by Bill Yenne
Captioned by Timothy Jacobs

Page one: An alert little Thoroughbred foal. *Pages
2–3:* A fine chestnut-colored saddle horse. *These
pages:* A Texas cowboy and his Quarterhorse — the
versatile descendant of English Thoroughbreds and
horses of Andalusian stock.

Picture Credits

All photographs courtesy of Robert and Eunice Pearcy
except:
American Graphic Systems Archives 8 (bottom), 12 (top),
   63 (top right), 156 (top right)
American Mustang Association
   Lenore Negri 99 (all)
American Paint Horse Association 108-109, 110 (top),
   113
Orville Andrews 12 (bottom)
Appaloosa Horse Club, Incorporated
   Darrell Dodds 28 (top)
   Betsy Lynch 26 (top), 28-29, 30-31
   Chris Olney 28 (bottom)
Australian Overseas Information Service
   J Brian 49 (left)
   Jim Fitzpatrick 48
   Michael Jensen 122
   Alex Ozolins 164
Austrian National Tourist Office 72 (all)
British Tourist Authority 10-11 (all), 58, 140-141
Brompton Books Archives 65 (bottom)
Gay Cole 100 (bottom)
©RE DeJauregui 52
Dover 6, 42, 178 (top)
Florida Division of Tourism 184 (right), 185
John Freeman 13, 50 (bottom), 56, 57, 70, 140, 174
   (bottom)
The Horse Magazine, Victoria, Australia 43, 165 (all)
Jim Huff 80 (top)
Kentucky Department of Travel Development 46, 70
   (right), 158-159 (all), 172, 173, 175 (top), 177, 180
   (bottom)
J&J Kidd 184-185

Las Vegas News Bureau 189
©Reverend MJ McPike Collection 71
The Minnesota Zoo 120-121 (all)
Morgan Horse Ranch
   Gina Muzinich 84 (all), 86-87, 88 (bottom), 90-91, 92
   (top), 94-95
National Archives 97
New York State Department of Economic Development
   152, 154 (top), 160 (bottom right), 174 (top), 175
   (bottom), 184 (left)
Palomino Horse Breeders of America 102
Peter Newark's Historical Pictures 45, 50 (top)
San Francisco Police Department 128 (top)
John Scott 51, 181 (top)
Southwest Spanish Mustang Association
   Gilbert H Jones 96, 98
Rolf Steinburg 162
Super Jock, Incorporated 62, 65 (top)
Texas Tourist Development Agency 14-15, 102-103,
   104-105, 134-135, 161
   OC Garza 4-5
   Michael Murphy 132 (bottom), 188 (top)
   Richard Reynolds 76, 154 (bottom), 156-157 (all)
TURESPAÑA, de la Secretaría General de Turismo 8
   (middle), 61 (right)
Harold Twitty 144, 145, 146 (all), 147, 148 (all), 149,
   150-151
Virginia Division of Tourism 8 (top), 34 (top), 38 (top),
   49 (top and bottom right), 54-55, 157, 170-171, 178
   (bottom), 179 (bottom), 180 (top), 182, 190-191
Sandy Wares 132 (top)
Wisconsin Division of Tourism 1, 44-45, 46-47, 106
©Bill Yenne 60, 64 (top left), 66 (top), 128 (bottom)

CONTENTS

INTRODUCTION

Above: **Nineteenth-century art of man and horse.** *At right:* **A Welsh Pony with bridle and bit. The breeding and training of horses has gone on for millenia.**

This book is written about, and dedicated to, the horses — all types — that have so faithfully served their owners and masters for thousands of years. Admittedly, the dog may be called 'man's best friend,' but for every dog that has given its life to protect its master's family, there are thousands of horses that have worked themselves to death at their master's bidding, or died with their master on the field of battle. Those of us who have used horses for various tasks throughout our lifetimes have seen the overworking, underfeeding and harsh treatment given horses by some people, even while these animals carried on the best they could.

One example of such mistreatment concerns the 3000 horses unloaded from freighters at Skagway, Alaska in 1897 and used to pack supplies over White Pass. Many writers of the the time claim that not a single horse survived more than a few weeks. We also have read that horses sometimes were worked without feeding until they dropped dead. Some say that such starvation could last for as long as 21 days. Others tell of horses being unpacked when hopelessly mired in a boghole, and left there alive to die. Fortunately, today there are laws, monitored by the Society for the Prevention of Cruelty to Animals (SPCA), that have put a stop to most of this mistreatment.

Horses have been an essential partner with mankind in the development of human civilization. For thousands of years — until well into the nineteenth century — almost all commerce on land was conducted through the use of horses, primarily fast saddle mounts that carried individual riders over long distances, or big draft animals that pulled or carried heavy loads.

The first record of domestic horses were of those used by the Hittites in Mesopotamia around 2200 BC to pull chariots, although there are indications that the Sumerians also used horses nearly eight centuries earlier. Over subsequent millennia, horses came to be domesticated by the people populating the vast region that stretches from Europe, across the Russian steppes, and into China. The Chinese of the Chou dynasty (1122 – 249 BC) used a small, fast steppe horse, from which today's Chinese and Mongolian breeds have descended.

When the Hittites introduced their Mesopotamian Nicaean horses into North Africa around 1370 BC, interbreeding with African types laid the groundwork for the Numidian horse familiar to Hannibal, and ultimately to the Barb and Arabian that we know today. These horses were later imported into Europe by invading Moors in the first millennium AD, and further interbreeding with the European 'Heavy Horse' led to the development of many of the fast, but sturdy, breeds we know today.

With the extinction of the prehistoric 'proto-horse' *Eohippus*, horselike animals generally ceased to exist in the Western hemisphere. But Christopher Columbus corrected this problem on his second voyage in 1494. Cortez brought 16 horses from Cuba to Mexico in 1519, and during the sixteenth century the Spaniards brought many more horses. From escaped domestic horses there came herds of feral (half wild) horses. Soon they were falling into the hands of the Indians as far north as the Canadian border. It was at this point that the Mustang began to evolve. The Indians, who had never before seen a horse, proved to be natural horsemen, and soon were riding them on buffalo hunts and during raids upon other tribes and during battles, and were using them as draft animals to pull travois. Indeed, the Nez Perce tribe played a key role in the development of the Appaloosa breed.

There were no horses in Australia until 1788. As in America, bands of feral horses developed from domestic ones that had escaped. The Aussies call these wild horses 'brumbies.'

The modern horse (*Equus caballus*, family *Equidae*) is descended from ancient horses that roamed the Earth 60 million years ago. The earliest forms are known from fossils dating to the lower Eocene period, and include the *Hyracotherium* of England and the *Eohippus* of North America. They were nearly identical, although the teeth of *Eohippus* showed more complexity. They stood roughly three hands high (twelve inches at the shoulder), with a short neck, toed feet and arched back. In the middle Eocene, the *Orohippus* developed, which was similar but roughly one hand larger, and which stood more erect like a modern horse. Further developments in the course of evolution

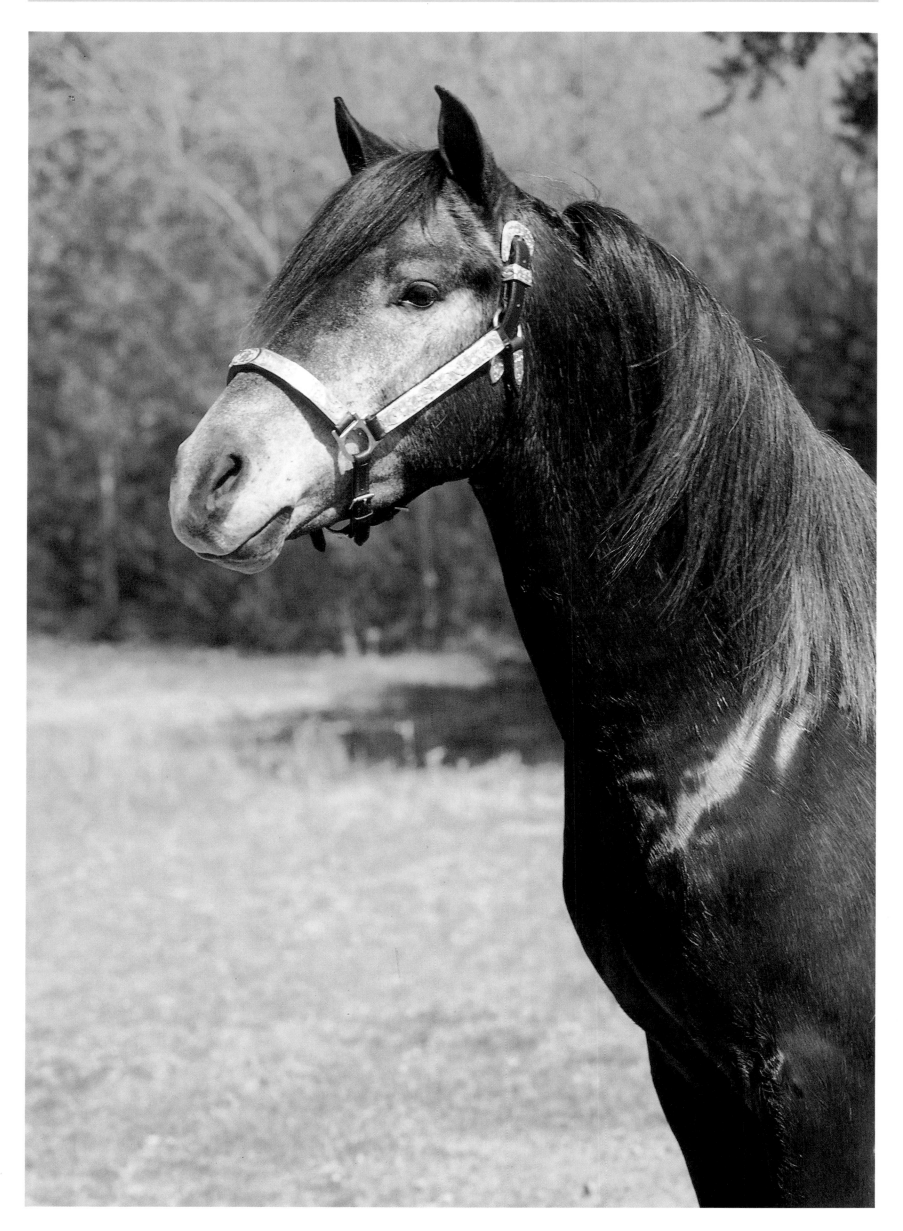

were the *Mesohippus* of the Oligocene and the *Merychippus* of the Miocene period. *Pliohippus*, which developed in the Pliocene period, was the first one-toed or hooved horse and, at ten hands, was about the size of the smallest of modern ponies.

Today, horses comprise the family *Equidae* within the order *Perissodactyla*. There are two species within *Equidae*: the *Equus prezewalskii* (the wild horse of Mongolia) and *Equus caballus* (all other horses). Today, there are well over 200 breeds within *Equus caballus*, although the exact number is obscured by precise definitions of the breeds. In other words, some authorities may define a type as a specific breed, while another may define it simply as being a subtype of another breed. Furthermore, some breeds are derived from other breeds and, as such, the two may be virtually indistinguishable. Some breeds are defined by a specific color, such as the Albino, Appaloosa or Palomino, while other breeds are defined by particular features, such as size or shape, and may be *any* color. For this book, we not only have tried to select well recognized breeds, but even obscure ones that may be considered by some to be subgroups of other breeds. We've also included semi-wild breeds, such as those found in southern Europe, central Asia and the Americas, that are harder to categorize.

In general, domesticated breeds can be categorized into three basic groups: pony breeds, sporting breeds and draft breeds. Ponies are the smallest, tending to stand no more than eleven hands. The Shetland is a typical pony. Other examples include the small (13 hands), rugged and semi-wild mountain horses of Southern Europe, such as the Skyros Bardigiano, Landais, Sorraia and Garrano.

The sporting breeds tend to account for the majority of all horses and are generally used as saddle horses or as pack and harness horses for light to moderate loads. These horses generally stand in the 12 to 15 hand range. The horses used for sporting events, such as racing and rodeos, are of this category, of which the Arabian, Thoroughbred and Quarter Horse are typical.

Although many draft horses are no taller than many sporting horses, they *can* range up to 17 hands or more, and are always heavier than a sporting breed of the same height. The 16 hand class draft horse is very common, and there are many such breeds, such as the Percheron, Belgian and Clydesdale, which have been developed in Northern Europe. Indeed, there are few draft breeds in the world which are not heavily influenced by an infusion of Percheron and Belgian blood. Draft horses are descended from the great medieval 'Heavy Horses' that were used to carry armor-laden knights into battle. They have been bred over the succeeding centuries to pull large, heavy wagons or machinery, either alone or in teams. While there is a great deal less of this type of work available for draft horses today than there was 200 years ago, draft horses almost certainly will remain gainfully employed at their ancient art indefinitely.

Below: **A comparison illustration of skeletal parts of horses from ancient times to the present. Contemporary breeds comprise both draught and saddle horses** *(these pages),* **including the elegant Arab (Spanish variant** *at right).*

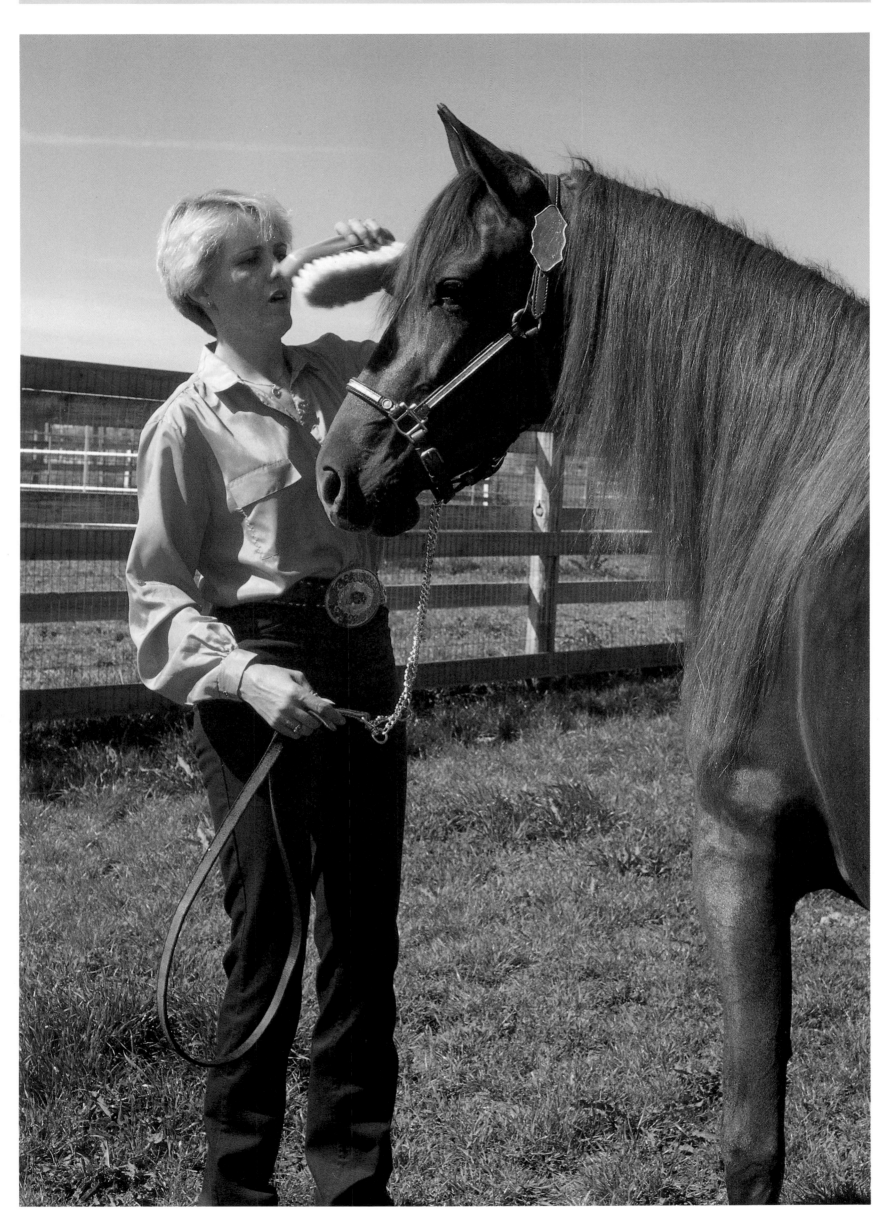

Today, there are roughly 50 million horses in the world. No worldwide census has been done, but a large number of these animals are known to be pure or nearly-pure breeds. Of the 5.5 million horse in the United States, for example, 84 percent are considered purebreds. The ten largest breeds in the US are:

1. Quarter Horse — 1,852,000
2. Arabian — 620,000
3. Thoroughbred — 533,000
4. Appaloosa — 258,000
5. Standardbred — 150,000
6. Paint — 147,000
7. Morgan — 127,000
8. Tennessee Walking Horse — 92,000
9. American Saddlebred — 89,000
10. Palomino — 23,000

The Quarter Horse is also the most common horse in Australia, with 50,000 animals on register. The Arabian is second in the land down under, with 40,000 horses listed in the breed registry. In England, the Thoroughbred is much more important than the Quarter Horse, and the Arabian is a common breed throughout Europe and, of course, North Africa. The large 16 hand class draft breeds are found throughout the world, but their greatest numbers are in northern Europe.

Horses are, indeed, to be found wherever there are people, serving their needs for a sturdy helper or as a pleasant companion on a Sunday ride, as they have for countless centuries. It is our hope that, in putting this book together, we have touched upon a large number of the types of horses in use today.

Below: Queen Elizabeth II arrives in the royal landau, on the first day of Royal Ascot, which remains one of Great Britain's premier social gatherings and equestrian events. *At right:* Two young British riders and their mounts.

THE HORSE'S AGE

A question the shoer will often be asked by the owner is, 'How old is that horse, or mule?' Here are clues to the answer:

A foal is born with 10 grinders. In about two weeks it will have four front teeth, two in the center above, and two in the center below. At two months it will have four more front teeth, outside the first ones. At eight months four more will appear at the corners of the jaw, outside the four the colt already has.

By the age of one year these corner teeth will have reached the height of the others. The colt will now have 12 front teeth, six above and six below. Each tooth will have a dark depression in its center.

By the age of two years this depression will be almost entirely ground out. In the colt's third year the middle front teeth are shifting, so that by the *end of its third year* these middle teeth have been replaced by the animal's first permanent front teeth.

By the age of four the colt has four permanent front teeth above and four below. Permanent teeth have by now replaced those between the center and the corner teeth. It still has colt teeth at the corners.

By age five these corner teeth have been replaced by permanent (adult) teeth, and the canine (bridle) teeth appear. All 12 of the front teeth will now have dark cups (kernels) in their centers. Horsemen refer to the five-year-old mouth as a 'full mouth' because of its having the bridle teeth as well as all of the cups. Some horsemen claim that this fifth year in a horse's life is a 'weak year,' especially in race horses, because of this double change. Others, of course, dispute this.

By the age of six the cups are gone from the two center teeth.

By the age of seven, the next two teeth have lost their cups, leaving only the bottom corner teeth with cups. In buying horses and mules for the US Forest Service and National Park Service it is a general rule not to buy an animal older than seven. Therefore, in making the first check of the age of a desirable animal, a glance at one of the lower, outside teeth is all that is needed to learn if the animal is past seven. If that tooth has a distinct cup the buyer knows that the animal is seven or younger.

At eight years the cups are gone from *all* of the lower front teeth, and at the end of that year *when the animal is nine* the cups are worn out of the two center upper teeth.

By age 10 the upper teeth between the center and corner teeth have also lost their cups, the cups in the corner teeth are on their way out, and the hook on the teeth has increased in size. Also, the bridle teeth have lost their points.

By the 11th year the last of the cups have disappeared.

By the time the *animal is 12* the crowns of the front teeth have become triangular and the bridle teeth have been somewhat worn down.

Horsemen will vary in their opinions as to which of these last three years mark the time at which the horse becomes a 'smooth mouth.' Some types of grazing can cause unnatural wear on the teeth, and can confuse the person doing the 'mouthing.' As the horse advances in age the gums shrink away from the teeth of the lower jaw, giving the teeth a narrow appearance. The centers of the teeth where the cups once were have a darkish point.

You may have heard that after the animal is nine years old a wrinkle appears in the corner of the lower eyelid, and every year thereafter an additional, well defined wrinkle will appear. For instance, a horse 12 years old would have three wrinkles, and so on.

Many horsemen will dispute this, but those that have made a study of it over the years and have learned to recognize the wrinkles have been able to prove its validity. Another method that this writer has heard of for telling the age of a horse is by a change in the spacing of the rearmost ribs in older horses. Some readers may too have heard of this method. The tooth method is, however, the universally accepted method for determining the age of the horse or mule.

DENTAL BATTERY OF AN ADULT HORSE

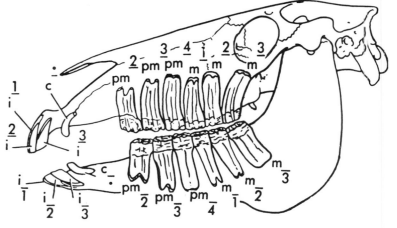

Skull and permanent teeth of a five-year-old horse: *i,* incisor; *c,* canine; *pm* premolar; *m,* molar.

Note: The size of a horse is traditionally measured in a unit known as the 'hand.' This originally meant and really still does that a person could quickly measure a horse by using his hand. Eventually, the 'hand' was standardized to four inches, or 10.16 centimeters. The figure to the right of the decimal in a 'hand' measurement is a number of inches, hence '.3 hand' is *not* 30 percent of a hand but three inches, or 75 percent of a hand. A horse that stands 15 hands is 60 inches tall, while a horse that stands 15.3 hands is 63 inches tall.

The measurement is made from the ground to the top of the animal's withers, a point at the base of the back of his neck between the shoulder blades.

The hand measurements given for each breed in this book are averages and are used to give the reader a general idea of the size of a given breed in relation to other breeds. In some cases, however, breed organizations will maintain particular height limits as definitions of their breeds. These may vary from continent to continent, but are within the parameters of the averages that we list.

At right: **The mounted band of the Queen of England's Household Cavalry prepares for a military pageant.** *Below:* **A Pinto grazing in a pasture.**

THE PICTORIAL

ENCYCLOPEDIA

ADAYEV (See KAZAKH)

AKHAL-TEKÉ

This breed originated in the Turkmen region of the Soviet Union and is now bred throughout central Asia. Used today primarily for racing and as a saddle horse, these horses range from bay to grey in color, and average 14.2 hands in height. One member of this breed, *Absent*, won the gold medal for dressage in the 1960 Olympics.

ALBINO

Not considered a distinct breed in much of the world, the American Albino started as a breed at the White Horse Ranch near Napier, Nebraska in 1918 with the white stallion *Old King*. He was so named because of his reputation as a sire of white- and pink-skinned foals. *Old King* himself was foaled in 1906 of unknown pedigree, but reportedly had the appearance of good breeding. In Nebraska he was mated with solid color mares of Morgan type and consistently produced foals that interested the White Horse Ranch owners, Caleb P Thompson and his wife, Ruth White Thompson. In 1937 the Thompsons founded the American Albino Association, which became the American White Horse Club in 1970. After Caleb Thompson's death, his wife resumed her maiden name (of Ruth E White) and continued with the breed at Crabtree, Oregon.

Technically, an 'albino' is defined as being a victim of *albinism*, ie, an animal having a congenital lack of normal pigmentation and characterized by having all-white skin and hair, along with red or pink eyes that are extremely sensitive to light. In the case of this breed, albino refers only to their having a pure white coat. Their eyes are pigmented, so there is no problem with light exposure.

These horses are registered on the basis of color, and ideally stand 14.2 hands. The Albino characteristic is found in many breeds of horses, especially the Palomino and Appaloosa. However, to be an Albino they must be pure white (or light cream) in color. Their breeding is principally for show and parade.

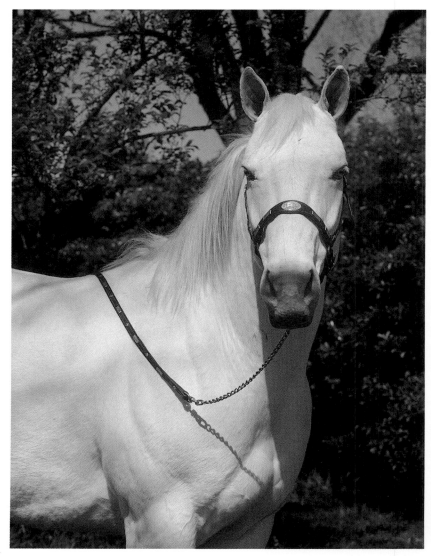

Previous pages: **An American cowboy and his steed.** *These pages:* **Albino horses, so named for their white coloration — not for the condition called albinism.**

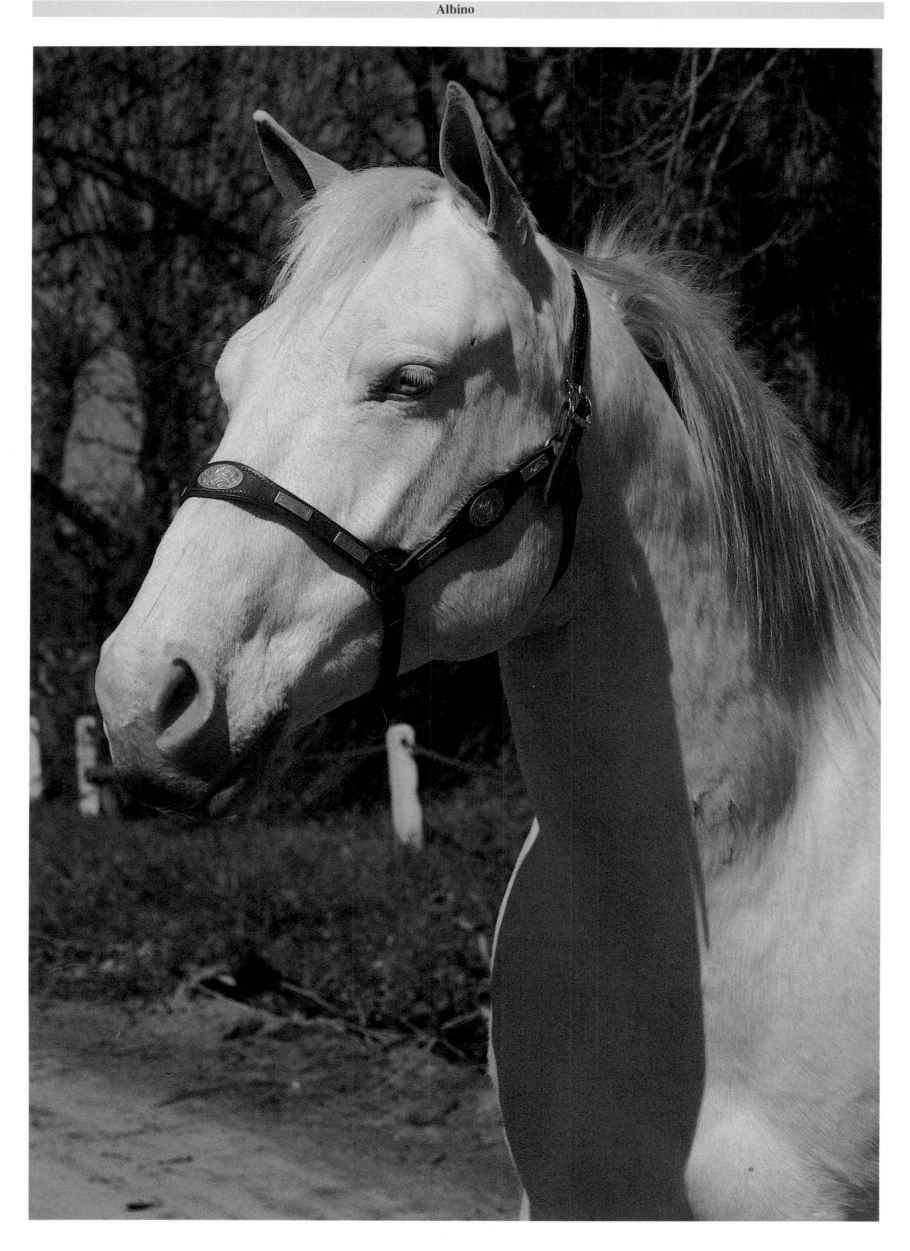

ALTÉR REAL

This little known breed was founded in the province of Alentego in southern Portugal by the House of Braganza at Villa do Portel in 1748 by using Andalusian mares and Arabian stallions. Eight years later the stud farm was moved to its present site, at Altér in Portugal, from which the breed derived its name. Altér ponies are best known as fine, spirited riding horses. Their coloring tends towards dark colors — brown or bay.

In its early years the Braganza Stud Farm encountered many bad times, including the theft of its best stock by Napoleon's troops in 1814. Later, much of the farm's land was confiscated when King Miguel abdicated in 1834. The breeding stock was reduced drastically, and the Royal Stud was abolished. The remaining stock was subjected to much infusion of Hanoverian, Norman, and later Arabian blood. In 1932 the Portuguese Ministry of Economy took over, and since then has greatly improved the breed by culling out unsuitable mares and using only the fittest of stallions. Their height ranges from 15.1 to 16.1 hands, and their color is mostly brown, bay or grey, with an occasional chestnut. Their neck is well arched; their body is short, coupled with fairly short legs and a small head.

AMERICAN SADDLEBRED

Although this breed was developed as a working horse, it is very much at home in the show ring, where it demonstrates its class in either the three-gaited or the five-gaited events. These extravagant events are encouraged by the use of heavy shoes and the extreme

Above right: **Sorrel and chestnut American Saddlebreds, and** *below,* **a side view of a chestnut Saddlebred.** *Opposite:* **A blaze-faced American Saddlebred.**

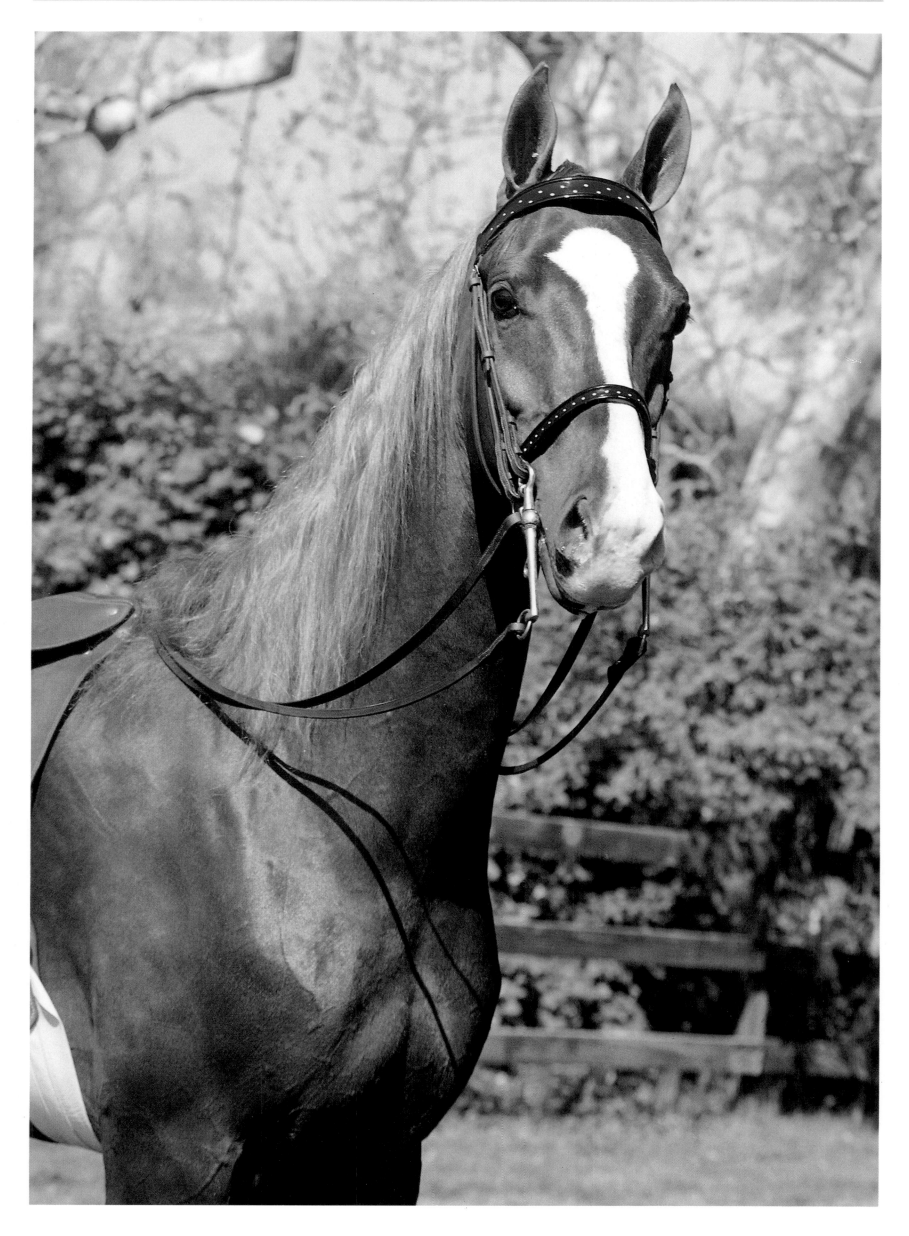

length of the hooves. Although their cantering movement is more up and down than forward, they can be incredibly swift, oftentimes running a mile in two minutes, 20 seconds. In spite of their fiery, high-strung appearance, Saddlebred horses are known to have one of the most amiable temperaments, and can be easily ridden or handled by children.

To achieve the requirements of this breed, the Kentucky breeders used Canadian and Narragansett pacers, crossed with good Morgans, Thoroughbreds and Arabians. The blood of the Thoroughbred *Messenger*, used in the development of the Standardbred, also played a major role in the development of the Saddlebred. The Canadian pacer *Tom Hall* also was considered a great sire in the breed's early days, although the stallion *Denmark* has been named as the official foundation sire.

The American Saddle Horse Breeders Society was founded in 1891 and is now located at Louisville, Kentucky. These horses range from bay to black, usually have white markings on their faces and legs and stand between 15 and 16 hands.

Below: **This American Saddlebred, with its very light mane, would also qualify as a Palomino. Note the very light golden color of its coat.** *At right:* **A very beautiful stripe-faced chestnut American Saddlebred, with white stockings.** *Overleaf:* **A dark bay American Saddlebred in motion.**

AMERICAN TROTTING HORSE

(See STANDARDBRED)

ANDALUSIAN

This breed of attractive, highly intelligent horses was developed in the Andalusian region of southern Spain, probably by crossing Spanish mares with the Barb stallions brought there by the invading Moors. Other theories of its origin associate the Andalusian with the wild *Equus ibericus* encountered by the Roman legions, or the Numidian mares introduced into Spain by the Cartheginian General Hasdrubal. The Carthusian monks are credited for furthering its development, and it dominated Spanish breeding stock from 1100 to 1600 AD. They were the cornerstone of the royal stables established by Philip II in 1571. Although small numbers of them are scattered throughout the world (Columbus brought a few to America), the majority of Andalusians is still found in Spain and best known in connection with classical dressage.

In Spain, the *Rejoneadores*, or mounted bull fighters, ride Andalusians. Crossed with Thoroughbreds, this breed inherits the extra speed required for this sport. Furthermore, the Andalusian can be easily trained for use in dance acts!

The Andalusian also has played an important role in the creation of Lipizzaners, which resulted from breeding Spanish mares and stallions that were taken to Lippi (near Trieste) in 1580. In fact, the Andalusian's influence on the equine world comes close to rivaling that of the Arabian, as it was used in developing the Holstein, Nonius, Würtenberg, and Hanoverian breeds.

The Andalusian stands about 15.2 hands and may be roan, black, gray or bay in color.

APPALOOSA

This horse's name is adapted from 'Palouse,' the name of the area in which it originated. The Palouse River drainage is an area encompassing northeast Oregon, southeast Washington and bordering the area in Idaho that was the traditional home of the Nez Perce Indian tribe. The pronunciation of the word 'palouse' became slurred to Apalouse, and eventually Appaloose, then Appaloosa.

It is thought that these horses came into the possession of the Nez Perce about 1730, although the Spaniards used the horses earlier.

Below: A spotted blanket Appaloosa colt with facial blaze. *At right:* An Appaloosa with typically mottled skin and a star on its forehead. Appaloosas are suitable for many leisure and/or work usages.

Early fur traders coming into the area saw the horses and referred to them as 'the Nez Perce's horses.' The Nez Perce valued these horses so highly that they would not sell or trade a single animal. They are credited as the first tribe to systematically improve a breed of horses. Some writers have credited the Nez Perce Indians with the development of the breed, but the horse's ancestry actually dates back much further. It is true, however, that Chief Joseph and his tribe of Nez Perce in eastern Washington and northern Idaho loved their Appaloosas, and no doubt tried to breed them so that they might perpetuate the Appaloosa coloring. After the Nez Perce were defeated and placed on reservations in 1877, the horses became scattered, and it was not until the 1920s that an effort was made to re-establish the breed.

An Oregon wheat rancher and horse breeder named Claude Thompson was instrumental in starting the movement to re-establish this breed. The Appaloosa Horse Club was organized in 1938 in Oregon, and now has its headquarters in Moscow, Idaho. The first 4932 horses registered are considered the foundation stock. Since then, both parents must be registered before an offspring can be recorded. However, there is now a provision for tentative registration

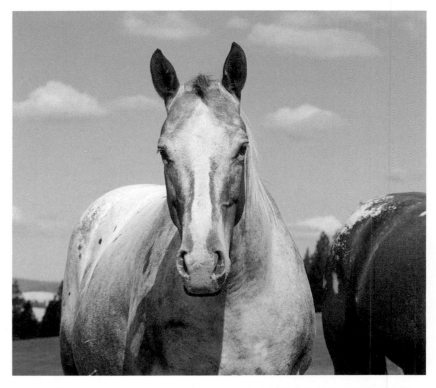

Below: **A spotted blanket Appaloosa colt.** *At far right:* **A snowflake Appaloosa with a star on its forehead.** *At right:* **A spotted blanket Appaloosa.**

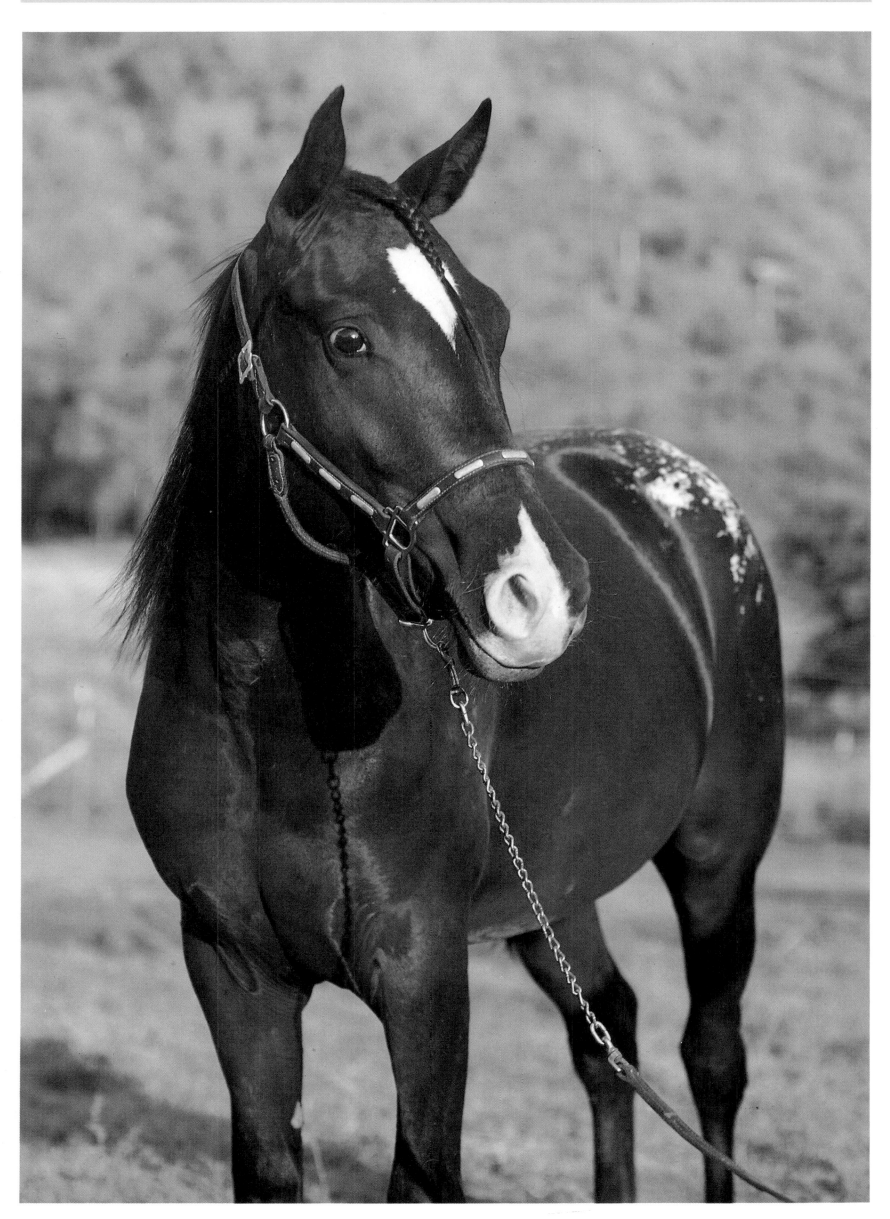

of an outstanding foal whose sire and dam are not registered. To be eligible, the horse must have Appaloosa breeding, have proper coloring, be of proper conformation, and be of desirable type. Horses of draft type, pintos or paints are not acceptable. Horses listed with this tentative registration may become permanent if, as a sire, they can produce twelve foals of desirable type. In the case of a mare, she must produce three such foals to achieve permanent registration. As with the Palomino or Pinto types, color is the most important feature in an Appaloosa. Therefore, they (see APPALOOSA PONY) may range widely in size, typically from 14.2 to 15.2 hands.

Nearly 80,000 had been registered by 1967, and in the past twenty years registration has escalated. The states of California, Idaho, Washington, Montana and Texas have had the most active registration.

Today, the registered Appaloosa horse must have mottled skin, which is most clearly seen around the lips, nostrils and genitalia. This skin will actually sunburn just like that of a fair-skinned human! It must also claim the distinctive white sclera in the eye. While not all spotted horses are Appaloosas, the six principal coat patterns that *are* considered in the registration of this breed are:

1. *Leopard* — Spots which are an opposite to the background color.
2. *Spotted Blanket* — A white rump and back with a dark background.
3. *White Blanket* — White overall.
4. *Snowflake* — White spots on any dark color.
5. *Marble* — Mottled all over the body.
6. *Frost* — Tiny white spots on a darker background, or vice versa, all over the body.

Appaloosas have good legs and chests, short backs and well-shaped necks, yet their tails and manes tend to be rather sparse and fine-haired.

Appaloosas, very prominent in all types of Western riding, are used both for pleasure and as work horses, and even make good roping horses.

Below: **Riders at an Appaloosa Horse Club steeplechase.** *At bottom:* **A rider on a white-faced snowflake Appaloosa.** *At right:* **A blaze-faced Appaloosa in harness to a gig, or cart.** *Overleaf:* **Getting ready to bridle an Appaloosa.**

APPALOOSA PONY

This diminutive Appaloosa is used primarily for Western riding. It was started as a breed in 1954, when Leslie Boomhawer of Mason City, Iowa acquired an Appaloosa mare that had a foal by a Shetland pony stallion. This very outstanding animal, named *Black Hand*, became the foundation sire of the new breed.

The Pony of America Club was incorporated in 1955. Within a decade, six thousand ponies had been registered, and over the next twenty years the breed flourished.

The herd books remained open for any Appaloosa colored pony which stands between 11.2 and 13.2 hands. No pony can be registered if its legs are white above the knees or hocks, or if it has a bald face. Ponies out of Pinto or Albino stock, or showing the color or markings of those breeds, also are barred.

ARABIAN (ARAB)

The Arabian holds an unchallenged position of leadership in the initial development of the horse world's finest breeds and their subsequent lines. Indeed, Arabian blood has been used at one stage or another to improve the quality of nearly every major horse breed that exists! Early history tells us that kings and emperors worshipped the liver chestnut colored Arabians.

Below: An Arabian mare and her leggy foal. *Above right:* An Arabian with classic gray coloring. *Far right:* An Arabian with an interrupted stripe and star on its face. Arabian blood has figured in every improved breed.

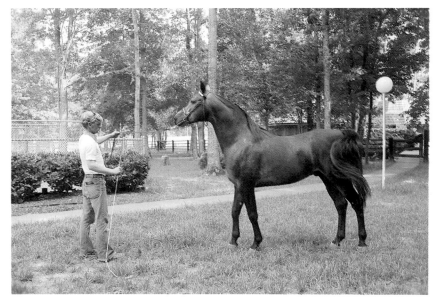

Pure bred Arabian horses are of solid color, bay, brown, grey, chestnut and sometimes white or black. White in the face and on the legs is common, but spots on the body are objectionable. Some of the Arabian's outstanding characteristics are its beautiful head and neck, bright clear eyes, well placed ears and large nostrils. The 'dished' shape of the face below the eyes is another important trademark.

Their pasterns are long and strong; their feet are slightly larger than other breeds' of comparable size. The Egyptian Arabian, regrettably, is no longer bred by the tribesmen in Arabia. This type tends to be slightly finer boned, and have — if such is possible — an even more refined and graceful head.

Not a large horse, the Arabian usually stands 14.1 to 15.2 hands high, but its physical endurance parallels no other breed in the world. Its most popular uses today are in Western and English riding, and as a show horse.

There is much speculation about the Arabian's origin, but Professor Sir William Ridgeway, who has done considerable research on the subject, suggests that the Arabian horse is a descendant of the wild Libyan horse that came from northern Africa and had been domesticated in Egypt centuries before the Christian era. Consequently, the people of North Africa have been breeding and improving the stock for many centuries. There is also evidence of the breed's existence on the Arabian peninsula as far back as 5000 BC. There,

Above: **A black Arabian at the Arabian Horse Farm in Virginia.** *Below:* **A blaze-faced Arabian colt, with white stockings.** *At right:* **A chestnut Arabian.**

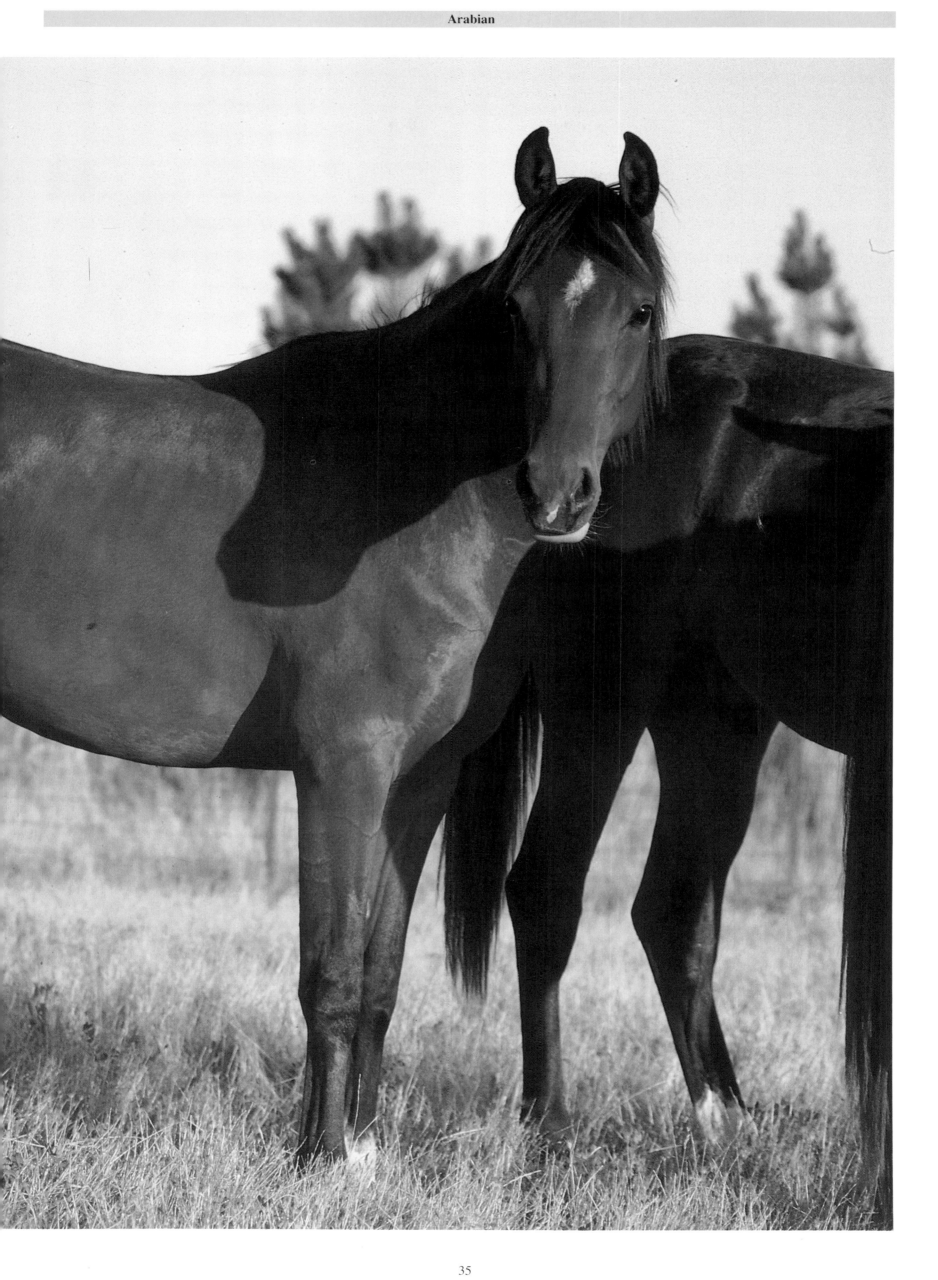

the Arabs jealously protected the purity of its blood for centuries, certifying that no foreign blood was ever introduced into the line.

Today, mention of the Arabian never fails to bring out a feeling of romantic mystique, associated with the rippling sands of the Arabian desert. The history of the wandering tribes of Bedouins are legendary. They developed a worldwide reputation as skilled horsemen and horse breeders, who held their horses in the highest esteem. For centuries, these people have depended on their horses in their everyday living, whether to care for their flocks, to plunder neighboring areas, or to ward off the enemy in desert warfare.

In England, Arabians strongly influenced the creation of the Thoroughbred. The foundation sires of the Darley, Godolphin, and the Byerley Turk breeds were imported in the seventeenth and eighteenth centuries.

The earliest account that we have of the Arabian's introduction to the United States is described by Homer Davenport in his books *Arab Horse* and *My Quest of the Arab Horse*. According to his account, the Arabian stallion *Ranger* was imported to America about 1765. This horse is said to have sired the grey horse that George Washington rode during the American Revolutionary War. Commander JG Elliot of the US Navy imported a consignment of both stallions and mares in 1838, and in 1856, Keene Richards imported two stallions and two mares. During and after the Civil War, however, Arabian blood became mixed with the American Saddlebred. In 1893, more Arabians were imported for the World Columbian Exposition in Chicago. Around the turn of the century,

Below: **A bay (chestnut body with black mane and tail) Arabian.** *At right:* **A bay Arabian with a classically Arabian mane.** *Above:* **Arabians trotting.**

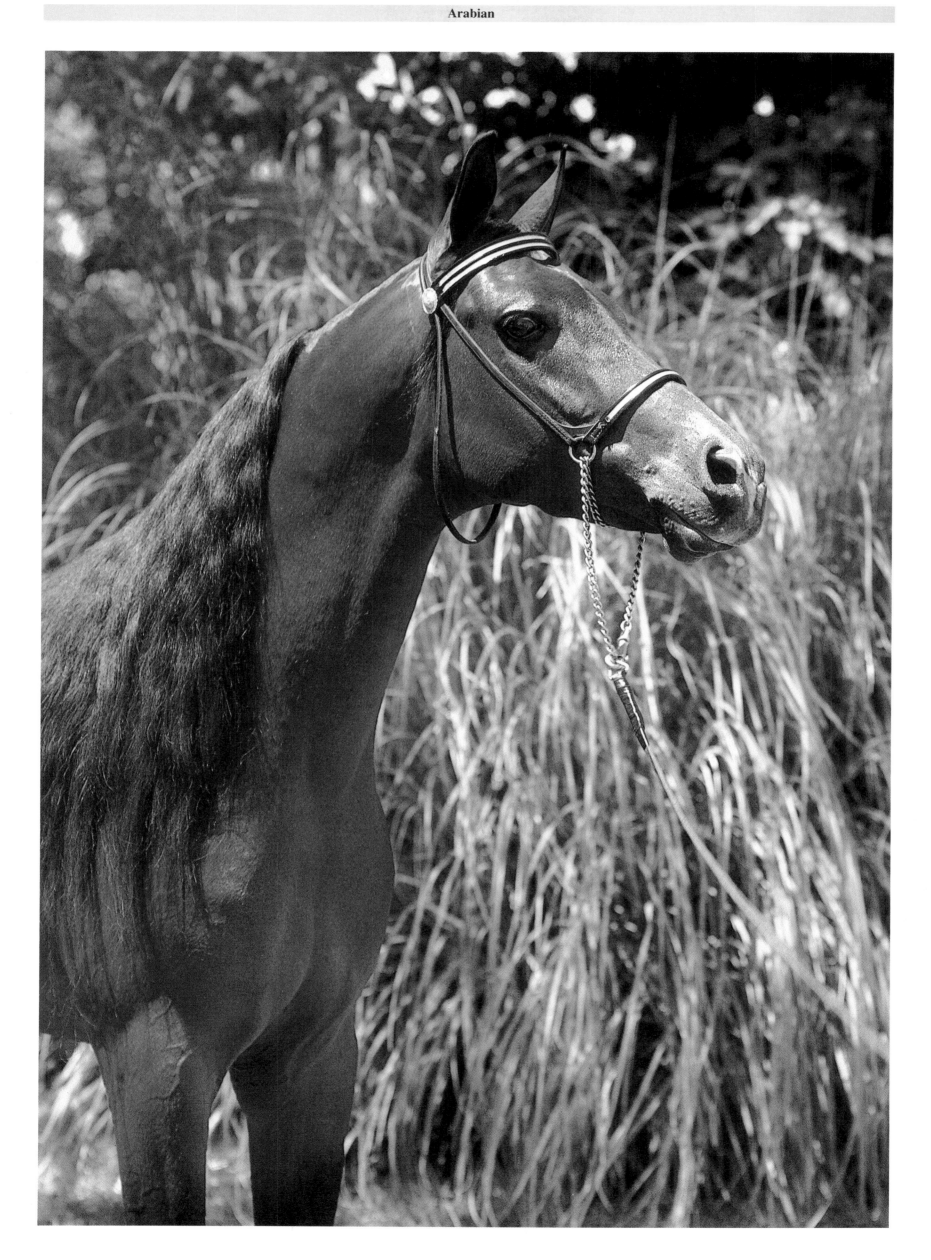

Davenport himself was one of the largest importers of Arabians. In 1906, he brought 26 head—and later many more—directly from the Arabian desert to his farm at Morris Plains, New Jersey.

Over the years, many horses have been imported from the Crabbet Arabian stud of England. The famous stallion *Crabbet* was owned by Wilfred and Lady Anne Blunt of Great Britain. Other famous English Crabbet studs are *Hanstead*, owned by Lady Yule, and *The Courthouse* stud, owned by HV Musgrove Clark. The famous Crabbet stallion *Aurab*, owned by Grace Baker of Aromas, California, has sired many very desirable stallions that are still standing at stud throughout central California. Like *Aurab*, all are liver chestnut in color. Other importers of the Crabbet line of Arabians include Spencer Bade of Fall River, Massachusetts; WR Brown of Berlin, New Hampshire; WK Kellogg of Pomona, California; and Roger A Selby of Portsmouth, Ohio.

The Arabian Horse Club registry of America was incorporated in 1908 in Chicago. By the late 1960s, over 40,000 Arabians had been registered, with 5340 of them in 1966 alone. In the last twenty years, registrations have accelerated as the number of Arabian horse owners has increased rapidly. There are probably more Arabian horse shows today than those of any other single breed.

Major Arabian subtypes include the Kuhailan, Munighi and Siglavy, which are a solid-colored Arabian bred in the Kirghiz region of the Soviet Union and known collectively as Strelets Arabians. These animals average 14.3 hands and are used under harness and as racehorses. Another subtype is the Yemen Arabian, originally bred in Yemen on the southern end of the Arabian peninsula and used today primarily as a saddle horse. The Shagya Arabian, native of Hungary, is all grey and stands 15 hands.

Above: A classic chestnut Arabian with a star on its forehead. *Below:* A bay on the run. *At right:* A very striking white Arabian stallion. *Overleaf:* A majestically beautiful bay stallion. Note the graceful, classic Arabian profile.

ARDENNES (ARDENNAIS)

As the name implies, this breed originated in the mountainous Ardennes region of France and Belgium, where it is thought to have been influenced by the horses brought north by Roman legions. Now related to the Belgian, this breed is used today, as it has been used through history, primarily as a draft animal. They have been used as breeding stock to influence many other breeds, and there are derivatives, though largely autonomous subtypes, known as Swedish Ardennes and Belgian Ardennes. These horses range in color from bay or chestnut, to sorrel or roan, and they average 15.2 hands in height.

ARIÈGEOIS (MÉRENS)

Native to the Ariège River drainage in southwestern France, this small, semi-wild breed is well-suited to the mountainous region in which it lives. Those which have been domesticated are recorded in a stud book established in 1948. They stand 14 hands on average and are almost always black.

ASSATEAGUE (See CHINCOTEAGUE)

ASTURIAN PONY (See GALICIAN PONY)

AUSTRALIAN PONY

This sturdy little (12 to 14 hands) pony was developed during the nineteenth century and was confirmed as a breed in its own right in 1931. The breed evolved from Timor ponies crossed with imported British stock (mainly Welsh Mountain Ponies), as well as Thoroughbreds and Arabians. One of the most significant foundation sires was the imported Welsh Mountain Pony, *Greylight*, who stood at Anthony Horden's Stud Farm in Bowral, New South Wales, in the early twentieth century. His influence on the breed is still well marked in today's ponies.

In recent years, two additional breed societies formed in an endeavor to breed ponies more suitable for riding by children. These organizations are the Australian Saddle Pony Association and the Australian Riding Pony Society. The aim of the latter is to breed finer types of ponies which resemble miniature Thoroughbreds.

AUXOIS

This breed originated during the Middle Ages in the Burgundy region of France and is used today primarily as a draft animal. During the nineteenth century, there was a strong Percheron and, later, Ardennes influence on the breed. This horse is typically bay or roan and averages 15.3 hands in height.

AVELIGESE PONY (See HAFLINGER)

BALI (See INDONESIAN)

BARB (BERBER)

A descendant of the ancient Numidian horse that served with Hannibal's legions, this breed originated on the Barbary Coast of North Africa, specifically Algeria. Barbs were introduced into the Roman Empire at an early stage and are thought to have been the principal horse used in chariot racing. They have subsequently been extremely important in the development of many other breeds, including such diverse types as the Andalusian, the American Mustang and even the Thoroughbred. The Libyan Barb is an important subtype, and those found in Spain are called Spanish Barb. These latter animals are used today primarily as saddle horses.

Barbs may range in color from dark bay or chestnut, to brown, black or grey. They average 14.2 hands in height.

BARDIGIANO (BARDI HORSE)

These small, sturdy animals probably originated in northern Europe but have been native to the Appennines of Italy since they were brought south centuries ago in the final assault that led to the fall of the Western Roman Empire. However, the breed was not officially recognized, and a stud book formed, until 1977. These horses range from bay to black, and may have small stars and limited leg markings. They average 13.2 and 14.2 hands in height.

The horses driven by the charioteer in the illustration *below* were in all probability Barbs. *At right:* An Australian Pony with bridle and bit.

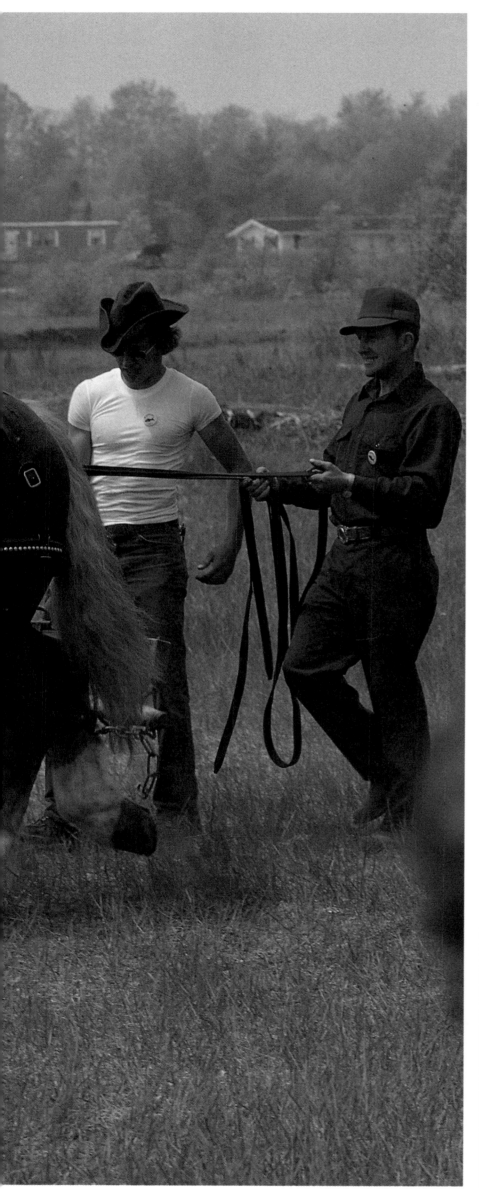

BASHKIR

This breed is one of the larger of the generally small class of steppe horses of central Asia, a class which also includes the Kazakh and Zemaituka. They have been influenced by larger riding horses, such as the Don, or still larger draft types, such as the Ardennes. Bashkirs range in color from bay to dun and typically stand 14 hands.

BARTHAIS (See LANDAIS)

BASQUE PONY (See POTTOCK)

BASUTO

This breed originated in the early nineteenth century in Lesotho (formerly the British colony of Basutoland) in southern Africa. It is probably derived from both Barb and Arabian stock introduced by European settlers. It was used in the Boer War and, over the years, as both a polo pony and race horse. Today, its primary use is as a saddle and harness horse. The Basuto may be any color and averages 14.2 hands in height.

BATAK (See INDONESIAN)

BELGIAN (BELGIAN HEAVY DRAFT)

A draft horse, this very attractive breed is a descendant of the Flemish Heavy Horse, which, in turn, dates to an ancient, now extinct heavy horse known from fossils found near Liège. Belgians are still very common in northern Europe and currently outnumber all other draft breeds combined in the United States. Through the centuries, the draft horses of Belgium grew in reputation, and the stud book for this breed was founded in 1885. In 1891, they were exported to the government stables of Russia, Italy, Germany, France and the old Austria-Hungary empire. However, after World War II, due to mechanization, the draft horse suffered a sharp decline. Today, their popularity is on the rise again.

The modern Belgian is a massive animal, but its beauty and attractive conformation somehow give it a distinctive appearance. For example, its legs and pasterns do not have the long, heavy hair found

Below: **British cavalrymen, riding Basutos in the Boer War of 1881.** *At left:* **A team of handsome Belgians in field harness.**

on the Shire and Clydesdale, which contributes to the latter breeds' thicker appearances. The Belgian is typically chestnut or bay in color.

Belgian stallions commonly weigh more than a ton and upwards to as much as 2500 pounds, with a usual height of nearly 17 hands. The mares most often weigh about 1800 pounds, with a height of 16 hands. They are powerful draft animals, and in pulling contests it is common for either a single animal or a team to pull 195% of their weight on a dead weight skid! Their color is bay, roan or chestnut, with the latter color most predominant. Generally, the Belgian disposition is good, but under certain conditions they can show extreme nervousness.

BERBER (See BARB)

BHOTIA (BHUTIA)

Native to the Himalaya mountain country of India and Tibet, this breed is similar to the Spiti and Tibetan breeds, and is used today by the people of that region primarily as a pack animal or as a saddle horse. These horses are usually, although not exclusively, grey or white, and stand 13 hands.

BITJUG

This breed originated in the Soviet Union, and is used today primarily for harness and as a saddle and draft animal. It ranges from bay or chestnut, to brown and black, and averages 15.3 hands in height.

BLACK HORSE (See SHIRE)

BORNU

Used primarily as a saddle horse, this breed originated in West Africa in the region of present-day Chad and Nigeria. It is grey with black legs, mane and tail, and varies in height.

BOSNIAN

As their name implies, this small, all-purpose breed originated in Bosnia, which is now part of Yugoslavia. They are predominantly of very dark color, such as black or dark brown, and average 13.1 hands in height.

Below: **Belgian Draft horses and admiring tourists at Kentucky Horse Park, in Lexington.** *At right:* **A team of Belgians in competition.**

BOULONNAIS

This breed originated in northern France, with specific derivation a matter of controversy. One school holds that they are descended from Numidian stock from Africa, while another traces them to Oriental horses brought to France after the Crusades. William the Conqueror took them to England in 1066. The breed's stud book was founded in 1886. Used today primarily as a draft animal, it is grey, chestnut or bay in color and averages 16.3 hands in height.

BOURGUIGNON

This medium-sized draft breed originated in France, and may be any color. It averages 15.3 hands in height.

BRABANT

Closely related to the Belgian, this large draft breed originated in the Netherlandish provinces of Brabant, which are now part of Belgium and Holland. They range in color from sorrel to a reddish roan, and average 17 hands in height.

BRETON

From France's Brittany region, this horse can trace its roots back to 2000 BC. During the Middle Ages the breed, under the name *Bidet d'Allure*, was used by nobility for long-distance riding, but today the Breton is used primarily as a draft horse. In 1909 the breed was subdivided into the Corlay, Postier and Grande Breton types, with the latter being the largest in size (up to 16 hands, on average).

This horse can be chestnut, bay or a reddish roan, and averages 15.2 hands in height.

BRUMBY

This breed of Australian wild horse is descended from the horses taken 'down under' by early settlers. Its color and size varies widely.

BUDYONNY

Natives of the Don River country of the Soviet Union, Budyonnys are named for Marshal Budyonny, a hero of the Russian Revolution, who developed the breed in the 1920s from Don and Thoroughbred stock for use as a military horse. These graceful animals are used today primarily as saddle and sporting horses. Usually chestnut but also bay or grey, they average 15.3 hands in height.

BURGUETE

This draft breed originated in Spain and is usually bay or black. Its height can vary considerably.

BURMESE (SHAN)

Bred in the Shan region of Burma, these horses are similar to — but coarser and slower than — the Manipuri of India. They were used by the British in Burma as polo ponies, but they are generally less reliable as a saddle mount than other small breeds, such as the Manipuri. Burmese are usually dark in color and stand about 13 hands.

Below: Australian stockmen gallop after a herd of Brumbies in Victoria. *Below right:* An Australian rancher tries to tame a Brumby.

CABALO CHILENO (A Chilean form of CRIOLLO)

CALABRESE

This tall breed originated in the Calabria region of Italy. Derived in part from Arabian stock and later influenced by Thoroughbred stock, it is used today primarily as a saddle horse. This horse varies in color, but averages 16 hands in height.

CAMARGUE

Descended from the prehistoric horse found in fossil form at Solutré in southern France, today this breed is native to the Camargue region on the Rhone delta. It has also benefited from North African stock. Registered only since 1967, this breed serves primarily as a saddle horse. It is usually grey and averages 14.2 hands in height.

CAMPOLINO (A Brazilian form of CRIOLLO)

CARPATHIAN

As the name indicates, this breed originated in the Carpathian Mountains of Eastern Europe, although it is principally associated with Poland. These dark colored animals are used today for many purposes. Small horses, they usually average 12.3 hands in height.

CARTHUSIAN

Originating in the area around Seville in Spain from Andalusian stock kept by the Carthusian monks of Jerez de la Frontera, these grey, chestnut or black mounts are used today primarily for harness and as saddle horses. These handsome and intelligent animals average 15.3 hands in height.

CASPIAN

Archaeological evidence shows that Caspians—perhaps one of the first breeds to be domesticated—existed in Mesopotamia in 3000 BC. They had been thought extinct until 1965, when a small herd was discovered in the wild in the Elburz Mountains of Iran near the Caspian Sea. They range in color from chestnut to grey and in size from 9.2 to 11.2 hands.

CHINCOTEAGUE (ASSATEAGUE)

Three hundred years ago a Spanish ship carrying horses was wrecked off the coast of the state of Virginia. These horses swam to Chincoteague Island, located along Virginia's northern coastline, where their descendants have lived ever since. Today, the Chincoteague Volunteer Fire Department sponsors an annual 'Pony Penning Day' as a fundraising event. Members boat their own mounts first to Assateague Island, where the drive begins, then ferry them through the water to Chincoteague Island, where they are penned. The next day, selected animals are sold for $50 to $250 at public auction.

The size of these horses has diminished over the years, until now their average height is less than 14 hands. These hardy ponies have naturally gentle dispositions, and can change from a wild state to docile pets within a few days, if handled properly. Therefore, they are not totally 'wild.'

Below right: Chincoteague/Assateague ponies in a herd during the annual roundup. *At bottom right:* Chincoteague/Assateagues evidencing piebald coats.

CHINESE

Native to the Gobi Desert area of China and Mongolia, this breed is used today by the people of the region as a general, all-purpose mount. Characterized by a long mane and tail, it is usually dun, with black points, and averages 12.3 hands in height. A small horse, it is obviously related to other semi-wild and domestic horses in central Asia, which has led to the assertion in some quarters that it is not a distinct breed, but an amalgam of Mongolian, Tibetan, Spiti, Manipuri and/or other regional breeds.

CHOLA

This all-purpose breed, a subtype of the Salteño, originated in Peru, and is usually dun in color. It averages 14 hands in height.

CLEVELAND BAY

The Cleveland Bay is a fairly large horse which was used in the not-too-distant past as a carriage horse. When crossbred with other breeds, most notably the Thoroughbred, it also serves as a fine riding horse. Purebred Cleveland Bays are good jumpers and hunters, again especially when crossed with Thoroughbreds. In crossbreeding, this horse is noted for its ability to pass on to other breeds the important qualities of substance, outstanding bone, good action, good color, hardness and endurance. Also known as both a draft and pack horse, this breed's color is mostly bay, with black points.

Fundamentally, it is a fine dispositioned horse, but can be spoiled if mishandled. Historically, it lays claim to being one of the oldest established English breeds, known at least since medieval times in the Cleveland district of Yorkshire, from which it takes its name. In Elizabethan times, with the use of coach travel, its traveling ability ensured that it would be much in demand. To this day, it is used as a carriage horse in the Royal Mews.

The Cleveland Bay is a traditional English breed. *At right:* **Cleveland Bays and Lipizzaners await the royal wedding party of Prince Charles and Lady Diana in 1981.** *Below:* **Queen Elizabeth II reviews the Palace Horse Guards.** *Above:* **The Duke of Cambridge on troop review in the nineteenth century.**

CLYDESDALE

The Clydesdale originated in the early eighteenth century in the Clyde River valley of Lanarkshire, Scotland. The stock was developed from several types of large English horses, with crosses of Flemish and Shire stock. The name was officially assigned in 1826 at the Glasgow Fair, and the Clydesdale Horse Society was founded in 1877. In general, the Clydesdale stands 16.2 to 17 hands. This makes the breed as tall as the Shire, but its build is less massive, its body not as heavy and its legs proportionately longer. Like the Shire, the draft horse's legs and pasterns are hairy—mostly on the back side—and its movements are fast and agile, belying its great strength and giant size.

The breed has long been known for its use in pulling brewery wagons, but nowhere have Clydesdales received more notoriety than as part of the famous 'Budweiser' team. When St Louis brewer Adolphus Busch, of the Anheuser Busch Brewing Company, created his famous 'Budweiser' brand in 1876, every brewery delivered its products in wagons pulled by huge draft horses, including Clydesdales. By the 1920s, most of the great draft beers were being delivered by trucks rather than by great draft horses.

However, to celebrate the end of Prohibition in 1933, August A Busch, Jr (grandson of Adolphus Busch) presented his father with a team of Clydesdales and a bright brewery wagon. It was the rebirth

of a proud tradition. Today, the Clydesdales are a living symbol of Anheuser-Busch, the largest brewer in the world.

There are three Clydesdale teams owned by Anheuser-Busch, and these operate out of St Louis, Missouri; Merrimack, New Hampshire; and Romoland, California. Each year they travel more than 60,000 miles and make up to 300 appearances, dazzling audiences with their precision, grace and power.

When the horses are in St Louis, visitors can see them as part of the Anheuser-Busch brewery tour. They are still housed in the original stables, which have been designated a national historic landmark. Summer visitors can also stop at Grant's Farm, just west of St Louis in St Louis County. There, they'll see the Clydesdale Breeding Farm, where 20 to 30 horses are born each spring.

Impressive in size and remarkable in precision, these gentle giants need plenty to eat. Each working horse consumes 50 to 60 pounds of hay and 25 to 30 quarts of feed a day. Their feed is a mixture of beet pulp, crimped oats, bran, minerals, salt, molasses and water—perfect for a hungry horse.

For Anheuser-Busch, the ideal horse is bay in color, 'has a blaze of white on the face, black mane and tail and, most importantly, white feathering on all four legs and feet.' However, the Clydesdale breed in general may also include dark brown or black horses as well. White markings are common. These animals stand 16.2 to 17 hands, although Anheuser-Busch prefers 18 hand Clydesdales for its teams.

Below: **The Anheuser-Busch/Budweiser Clydesdales and exhibition brewery wagon.** *At right:* **A white-faced Clydesdale.** *Overleaf:* **A stallion and colt.**

COB

The Cob is a type rather than a breed. There is no sure way of breeding to the Cob type, but it is most likely to be achieved by crossing a heavy draft horse with a Thoroughbred type. Its powerful hind quarters ensure some jumping ability, and it undertakes any task willingly and safely.

This type of Cob should not be confused with the Welsh Cob, which is a distinct breed in its own right, although Welsh Cobs have been used in the production of horses of the Cob type. Its height averages 15 to 16 hands, with generous quarters; a small head; strong, arched neck; short body and legs. A graceful horse for its size, it is known as an ideal riding horse for the less experienced or elderly rider because of its placid nature and impeccable manners.

COMTOIS

This large, yet lively, draft breed originated in southeastern France as early as the sixth century, and averages 15.3 hands in height. This horse is usually bay or chestnut, with a light mane and tail.

CONNEMARA

The only pony native to Ireland, the Connemara boasts the beauty of the Arabian, as well as the strength and hardiness of the Mountain Pony. The breed has been influenced by Arabian, Thoroughbred and Fjord stock. It is found in the wild along the northeast coast of County Galway, but can quickly be tamed into a gentle, well-behaved animal in a matter of a few days. The Connemara Stud Book was established in 1924.

Usually standing no more than 14.2 hands, the Connemara excels in jumping events, often outjumping horses of 16 and 17 hands. The great Connemara jumpers included *Little Squire*, who stood 13.2 hands — average for the breed — but consistently cleared seven foot jumps, while carrying a 160 pound rider. Another horse, *Nugget*, stood 15 hands. At the International Horse Show at the Olympic in London in 1935, he cleared seven feet, two inches to win the event. The great Connemara jumper *Dundrum* won the jumping competition at the Royal Dublin Horse Show for four straight years, competing against the finest jumpers in Europe. His greatest year was 1963, when he won the Aga Khan trophy, the King George V trophy, plus other world class meets, and was proclaimed 'King of the World's Jumping Horses.'

CORLAY (See BRETON)

CRIOLLO (MANGALARGA)

A Brazilian form of Mangalarga, this breed was developed in South America from horses imported by the Spanish in the fifteenth

At right: **An Irish Gypsy caravan with a Connemara in its traces.** *Below:* **A Connemara grazes on the bank of a lough near Maam Cross in County Galway.**

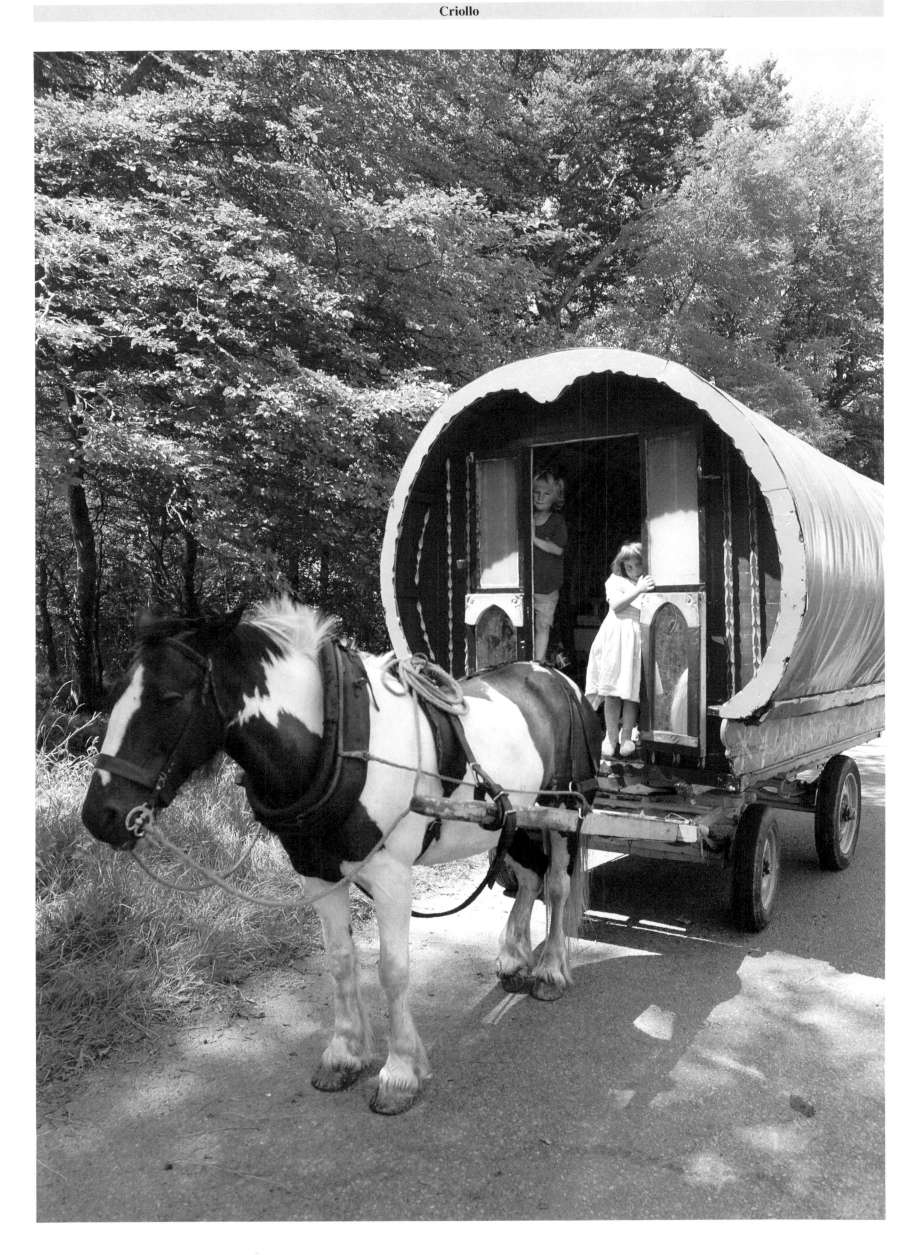

century. The Criollo is today also known as Caballo Chileno in Chile, Buajira in Columbia, Llamero in Venezuela, and Peruvian Paso (Peruvian Stepping Horse) in Peru, with the Morochuco of the Andes and the Crioulo, Mangalarga and Campolino (all of Brazil) and Costeño (of Peru) being major subtypes. It is used today primarily as a saddle horse. These horses may be any color, but usually tend to have white markings, although the Mangalarga subtype of Brazil is generally solid gray, roan or chestnut. They average 14 to 15 hands in height.

CRIOULO (A form of CRIOLLO)

DALES PONY

A British native breed that makes a perfect family pony, the Dales Pony is quite docile by nature and thus easy for children to ride. Because it claims great sturdiness for its size, which ranges up to 14.2 hands, this pony is suitable for adults to ride as well. At the present time the Dales Pony is used mainly as a pleasure saddle animal, but not long ago fulfilled man's needs as pack and draft animals.

Although its shape limits its speed, it is an excellent jumper. It also makes a superb mount for cross country trekking and does well in harness. Its hardy constitution enables it to live outside in the harsh weather so prevalent in northern England.

The Dales Pony takes its name from an area of north Yorkshire, where it has been bred in Durham and Cumbria counties for centuries. Until the end of the nineteenth century, it had never been recognized as being a breed separate from the Fell Pony (See FELL PONY). The Dales breeders credit the Welsh Cob *Comet* with having a permanent influence on the breed. *Comet*, a strong, heavy animal, was foaled in 1851, then taken from Wales to Westmoreland, where he competed in trotting races. He once covered 10 miles (six km) in 33 minutes, carrying 10 stone (140 pounds, or 63.5 kg).

DANUBIAN (See PLEVEN)

DARASHOURI (SHIRAZI)

Persia is the native land of this large and dashing saddle breed, and the breed is still common to the region. These horses are commonly chestnut, bay or brown in color, but may also be grey. They average 15 hands in height.

DARBOWSKO-TAROWSKI

(See WIELKOPOLSKI)

DARTMOOR

This small breed originated in England and has been a registered breed since 1899. Derived from the Thoroughbred, the Dartmoor is used today primarily as a saddle horse. It is usually black or brown, and averages 12.2 hands in height.

DEMI-SANG

A native of France, this large horse is bred today primarily for harness racing, although it is also commonly used as a saddle horse. It may be any color, and averages 16.2 hands in height.

DISEX

These small semi-wild mountain horses existed in the Pyrenees until roughly the time of the Spanish Civil War, in the late 1930s when they became extinct. They had a short mane, zebra-like markings, and were probably related to the ancient wild horses of prehistoric Europe.

DOLE (DOLE TROTTER)

This breed originated in Norway and is used today primarily for harness racing. These horses are black, brown or bay, and average 15.1 hands in height.

DOLE GUDBRANDSDAL

Not to be confused with the larger Dole, this breed also originated in Norway, but in the twentieth century. The breed's registry dates from 1941, and it is used today primarily as a draft horse, although it also has been used as a trotting horse. It is black or brown, and averages 15 hands in height.

DON

This sturdy and handsome breed originated in the Don River country of the western Soviet Union, and was greatly influenced in the eighteenth century by Turkmene stock and in the nineteenth century by Thoroughbreds. It is one of the most important breeds in the Soviet Union today, and is used primarily as a saddle mount. The Don is always always of solid color, although that color may vary, and averages 15.2 hands in height.

DONGOLO

Primarily a racing horse, this breed originated in Ethiopia. This horse may vary in color, as well as in size.

DÜLMEN

This small horse originated in Germany, and today lives in a generally wild state in the more remote parts of the Meerfelderburch of Westphalia. It ranges from bay to roan in color, and averages 12.3 hands in height.

DUTCH WARM BLOOD

This multitalented breed was established in the Netherlands in 1958, and has not yet gained the full recognition that it deserves. As its name suggests, the Dutch Warm Blood has earned a reputation as a versatile, reliable, high quality animal which is suitable for all types of riders. In harness, the Dutch Warm Blood has won countless coveted national and international show championships, both singly and in four-horse hitches. The 1982 Valvo World Cup winner, *Calypso*, ridden by Melanie Smith for the United States, was a Dutch Warm Blood.

The Dutch Warm Blood is based on two much older breeds, the Groningen and the Gelderland. The Groningen is used for the dual purposes of farming and carriage, and the Gelderland is a lighter type. These two older breeds were, in turn, crossed with well selected Thoroughbreds, with the aim of producing a fine looking animal, with good size and disposition, and a strong constitution. This horse averages 16 hands in height, and ranges in color from bay to chestnut, and from black to grey.

DZHABE (See KAZAKH)

Below: **Dartmoor ponies grazing in Dartmoor, Devonshire, England.** *At right:* **A Criollo type also known as 'Peruvian Paso' or 'Peruvian Stepping Horse.'**

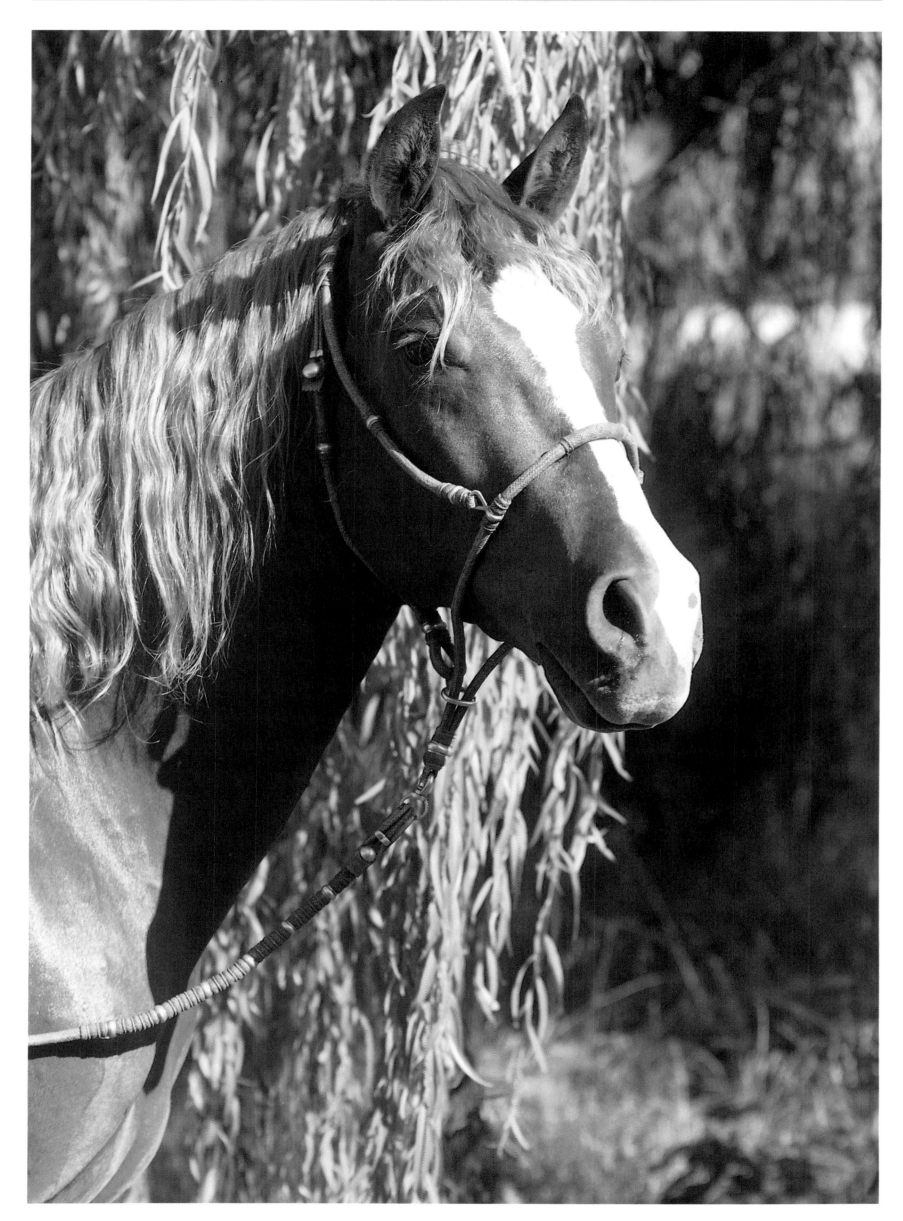

EAST FRIESIAN

This large breed originated in northern Germany in the coastal Friesian region, and developed in parallel with the closely related Oldenburg until World War II. After that time, Oldenburg development continued in East Germany, while East Friesians were bred in West Germany. The breed is used today primarily for harness and as a saddle horse. It ranges in color from bay to black, and averages 16 hands in height.

EAST PRUSSIAN (See TRAKEHNER)

EASTLAND (See NORTH SWEDISH)

EINSIEDLER

These horses originated at a Benedictine monastery in the Swiss canton of Schwyz, perhaps as early as 1064. They have had subsequent infusions of Hackney blood, and are used today primarily for harness and as show jumpers. They range from bay to chestnut in color and average 16 hands in height.

ELBURZ

This breed originated in the Elburz Mountains of Persia, on the southern shores of the Caspian Sea, and is used today both as a saddle horse and pack animal. It is varied in color and averages 12 hands in height.

ERMLAND

This chestnut draft horse originated in Poland. It averages 15.3 hands in height.

EXMOOR

The oldest pony breed in the United Kingdom, the Exmoor has probably existed in southwestern England since prehistoric times when the country was connected to Europe. Used as a pack horse and as a war horse by the ancient Celts, the little Exmoor is used today for pulling carriages and for children's pony rides. The Exmoor stands 12.3 hands and is brown or dun-colored, with a light-colored muzzle and belly.

FELL PONY

Bred mostly in the Pennine range of northern England, this pony is not built for speed, but recently has come into its own due to an increased interest in show driving. Originally, the Fell Pony came from the west side of the Pennine range; the slightly larger Dales Pony from the east side. Boggy or rocky terrain, fences and other obstacles do not deter this pony in its cross country travels. For driving they are superb, as their draft background has made them into strong pullers. This pony ranges from 13 to 14 hands and is usually dark in color. The Fell Pony Society, established in 1900, generally doesn't recognize animals with more than a trace of white markings.

History tells that this small pony was present when the Romans arrived in northern Britain. To improve its size, the Romans imported Friesians for cross breeding. Legend also tells how *Lingcrapper*, founder of an important strain of Fell, came to notice. He was found, saddled and bridled, after a border skirmish, his rider dead. The farmer who found him put him to stud for the remainder of his life.

FRANCHES-MONTAGNES

Developed in the Bernese Jura region of Switzerland during the latter part of the nineteenth century, this breed is used as both a

Below: **A driver and several carriages complete with Galiceño carriage horses await the tourist trade in downtown Guadalajara, Mexico.**

riding and light draft horse. This horse is influenced by Arab, Ardennes and Thoroughbred stock. It ranges in color from bay to chestnut and can stand up to 15.2 hands high.

FJORD PONY

A direct descendant of the wild horses of the ice age, this breed is mostly of dun (buckskin) color, with a dark eel stripe down its back and numerous zebra stripes upon its legs. Its mane and tail are black and silver, and its height never exceeds 14.2 hands. For most of the year, the Norwegian Fjord Pony's coat is long and heavy. In its native Norway the pony is used primarily as a farm horse, usually in harness, while in other countries the pony is commonly ridden.

FREDERIKSBORG

This tall breed originated in Denmark in 1562 during the reign of King Frederik. It was traditionally a court and riding school horse, and is used today primarily for harness, saddle or draft. These chestnut-colored horses average 15.3 to 16 hands in height. The Knabstrup, Orlov and Lipizzaner are descended from this breed.

FREIBERGER

This solid-colored breed originated in Switzerland, and is used today primarily as a show horse, both as a jumper and in harness racing. This horse averages 15.3 hands in height.

FRIESIAN (HARDDRAVER)

A relative of the East Friesian, this horse orginated in medieval times in the western, or Dutch, islands of the Friesian Archipelago that the Netherlands share with Germany. Originally a war horse, it is used today as a draft breed. It averages 15 hands in height and is black, with rare instances of white facial markings.

FRENCH TROTTING HORSE

The sleek and handsome French Trotter was carefully developed during the nineteenth century with Hackney, Thoroughbred, Standardbred and Orlov heritage. The latter, also well known as trotting horses, remain very similar to the French Trotter. The original trotting races for which the breed was developed were held at Cherbourg in the province of Normandy (after 1836), and hence, the breed is often referred to as a Norman trotter.

At the time the stud book was officially established in 1922, all but a handful of French Trotting Horses were descended from just five foundation sires. These were *Conquérant* (1858), *Lavater* (1867), *Normand* (1869), *Niger* (1869) and the great and stunning bay *Phaeton* (1871), who was himself descended from the great English Thoroughbreds *Sampson* (1745) and *Orville* (1799). One of the great French Trotting Horses today is *Minou du Donjou* (1978), who set a world speed record of 1:07 over a five kilometer course in Stockholm in 1985.

Since 1941, the breed has been rigidly limited to only those horses which meet the strictest criteria. The horse must be bay, chestnut or black and stand between 15.1 and 16.2 hands.

FULANI

This all-purpose breed originated in the Cameroon area of West Africa and averages 14 hands in height.

FURIOSO – NORTH STAR

This large, trim breed originated in the middle nineteenth century at the Mezöhegyes stables in Hungary, and is used today primarily for harness racing and as a saddle horse. It ranges in color from bay to black and averages 16 hands in height.

GALICEÑO

Used today primarily as a saddle horse, this breed was developed in Mexico from Spanish Garrano stock. This horse ranges in color from bay or sorrel to black, and averages 12.3 hands in height.

GALACIAN (ASTURIAN) PONY

A small, semi-wild horse remotely related to the extinct Disex, the Galacian is found in the mountains of Spain. This breed is occasionally domesticated for farm work in the region and also can be ridden. It ranges from black to brown and stands as tall as 13.1 hands.

GARRANO (MINHO)

An ancient horse — drawings are found in Paleolithic cave paintings — this semi-wild breed evolved in the mountains of Portugal. It is usually chestnut and averages 12.2 hands in height. This breed has probably had some infusion of Arabian blood since.

GARRON (See HIGHLAND PONY)

Below left: An Exmoor Pony at ease in a sunny pasture. *Below right:* A Galacian Pony at pasture near a magnificent Mediterranean coastline.

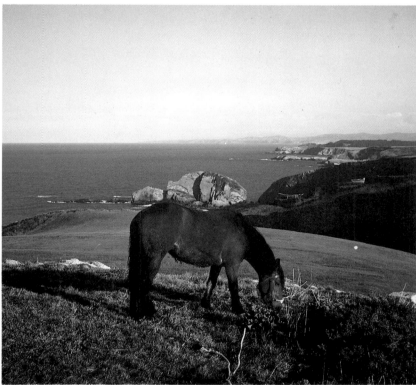

GELDERLAND

This grand horse derives its name from the province of the Netherlands, where it was first bred during the nineteenth century. Native mares were crossed with Norfolks and Normans, and later, infusions of Hackney and Oldenburg blood were made, which produced a very strong, active animal with good appearance. These characteristics have been passed on to the Dutch Warm Blood, a breed in whose development the Gelderland has played a major role.

The Gelderland is a stylish animal, most popular as a carriage horse. Since 1960, however, the Gelderland has been bred less and less because of the increased popularity of the Dutch Warm Blood. It stands 15.2 to 16 hands and ranges in color from chestnut or bay to black or grey, with white markings common.

GIDRAN

This large chestnut breed originated in Hungary and is used today as a saddle horse or as a draft horse. It averages 16.1 to 17 hands in height.

GOTLAND (SKOGSRUSS)

Still found in a wild state in the Swedish forest preserve at Lojsta, this breed originated in Sweden and is used today primarily as a racing or trotting horse. The Gotland varies widely in color from black or brown, to chestnut or grey, and averages 12.1 hands in height.

GREAT HORSE (See SHIRE)
GRONINGEN

This breed originated in the area of the Netherlands from which it takes its name, and is probably descended from Friesian and Oldenburg stock. Closely related to the Gelderland, the Groningen is today quite rare. It is used both as a saddle and draft horse, and is black or brown, averaging 15.3 hands in height.

GUAJIRA (A form of CRIOLLO found in Colombia)

HACKNEY

When this breed was developed in the eighteenth century, it was primarily an English saddle horse. When the roads in the Yorkshire were improved, however, the need for fast carriage horses sky-rocketed, and this development hastened the Hackney's transition to fine-harness driving. Since that time, the name of the breed has become synonymous with the highest class of carriage horse.

Like so many other fine breeds, the Hackney traces its ancestry back to the Thoroughbred and, of course, the Arabian. On average, this horse stands about 15 hands, making it smaller in size than the Thoroughbred, but larger than the Arabian. The Hackney may range from chestnut to black and often has white patches on its face and legs.

A horse known as the *Shales Horse*, foaled about 1780, is given credit for setting the pattern of this breed. He is said to have

Below: A Hackney Pony with a 'Super Jock' remote control jockey in the saddle.
At right: Gelderlands graze in a Holland pasture.

contained much Thoroughbred breeding, and was only four generations removed from *Darley Arabian*. The Hackney Stud Book did not, however, exist until 1883. In his book, *Hackney Horse*, John A Craig claims that the first Hackney brought to the United States was the horse *Bellfounder*, imported by James Booth of Boston in 1822. A daughter of *Bellfounder* was the mother of *Hambletonian 10*, the great foundation sire of the Standardbred. The Hackney Pony, a 13 hand variant of the Hackney with Fell blood, was officially recognized in 1880.

HAFLINGER (AVELIGNESE PONY)

This sturdy pony gets its name from the village of Haflinger (Avelengo) in the Italian Tyrol (formerly Austrian). Some experts contend that it originated during the fourteenth century during the reign of Holy Roman Emperor Ludwig IV, but others date it from the sixth century at the time of the Ostrogoth retreat from the Byzantines. While its actual ancestry has not been ascertained, the present breeding line began with the sire *Folie* in 1874, son of *El Bedavi XXII*, an Arabian stallion.

A mountain breed, the Haflinger is markedly similar in appearance to other mountain horses and is extensively used by farmers and foresters in Austria, Bavaria and Italy as a draft and pack animal.

Presently, the pony has discovered a new role, taking tourists and their gear on treks through the Tyrolean countryside. Queen Elizabeth II of England was presented with a pair during a visit to Austria.

HAILAR (See MONGOLIAN)

HANOVERIAN

The Hanoverian claims the singular honor of being Germany's most well-known breed. The breed is probably descended from the Great Horse of the Middle Ages, but the earliest official records date back to 1714 when George I of England — who was also Elector of Hanover — introduced British Thoroughbred blood into the German studs.

This horse ranges in color from chestnut to black to grey, with white markings being very common. Because of many crosses with the Thoroughbred, each horse varies greatly in size. A Hanoverian stallion usually reaches a height of 16.2 to 17 hands.

The breed has a long history of show performance in jumping and dressage, and is also widely used in international carriage competitions, where it has accumulated several championships. Famous Hanoverians include *Warwick Rex*, individual gold medalist at the 1976 Olympics, and *Simona*, ridden by the late Harwig Steeken at the men's World Championship. Gerd Wiltfang's world championship winner, *Roman*, is a Westphalian, a Hanoverian type bred in the Federal German State of Westphalia.

HARDDRAVER (See FRIESIAN)
HEAVY HORSE, OLD ENGLISH

(See SHIRE)

HEILUNG CHIANG (See MONGOLIAN)

Below left: Hanoverians grazing. *Below left, bottom:* A Hanoverian stallion.
Below right: A Hanoverian with an 'open' stance.

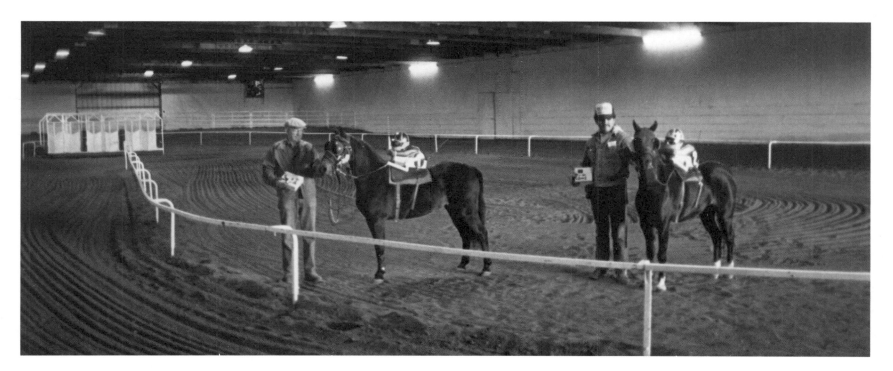

Above: Hackney Ponies with remote control jockeys and trainers at an indoor track. *Below:* England's King George II, on a Hanoverian.

HIGHLAND PONY

As the name suggests, this strong, calm-dispositioned pony claims Scotland as its homeland. This pony is graced with a very generous, fine-haired mane and tail, and its height averages 13.2 to 14 hands. The coloring varies from light grey and dun to bay, brown and black, and almost all Highland ponies have a darker dorsal eel stripe down the back.

Highland owners use this breed in a variety of ways, as draft or pack horses. Placed in harness, the pony can even pull a plow or wagon. In the course of its development, the Highland Pony has been crossed with Arabians, giving it a refined appearance.

HOLSTEIN

The Holstein is another of Germany's warm-blood breeds, which can reach 16.2 hands in height. Originally bred in the state of Schleswig-Holstein under standards laid down in 1680, it is of Oriental and Andalusian ancestry. Like the Hanoverian, this horse is also descended from the Great Horses of the Middle Ages, which carried knights in armor to battle. More recently, with the increased popularity of saddle animals, Thoroughbred blood has been introduced, making this large horse quite bold and very handsome, though it still retains its reputation as a sensible animal.

Meteor, one of the great show jumpers of the post-war years, ridden by Fritz Thiedemon, was a Holstein. The brilliant dressage horse *Granat*, ridden by the Swiss rider Christine Stuckleburger, has been in a class of his own for a number of years. Most Holsteins average a little larger than many riders would feel is necessary, but their versatility and temperament make them excellent all-purpose animals.

Above: Holsteins, renowned as saddle horses, on parade in West Germany. Note the flaring nostrils of the Holstein *below*. *At right:* A closeup of a Holstein.

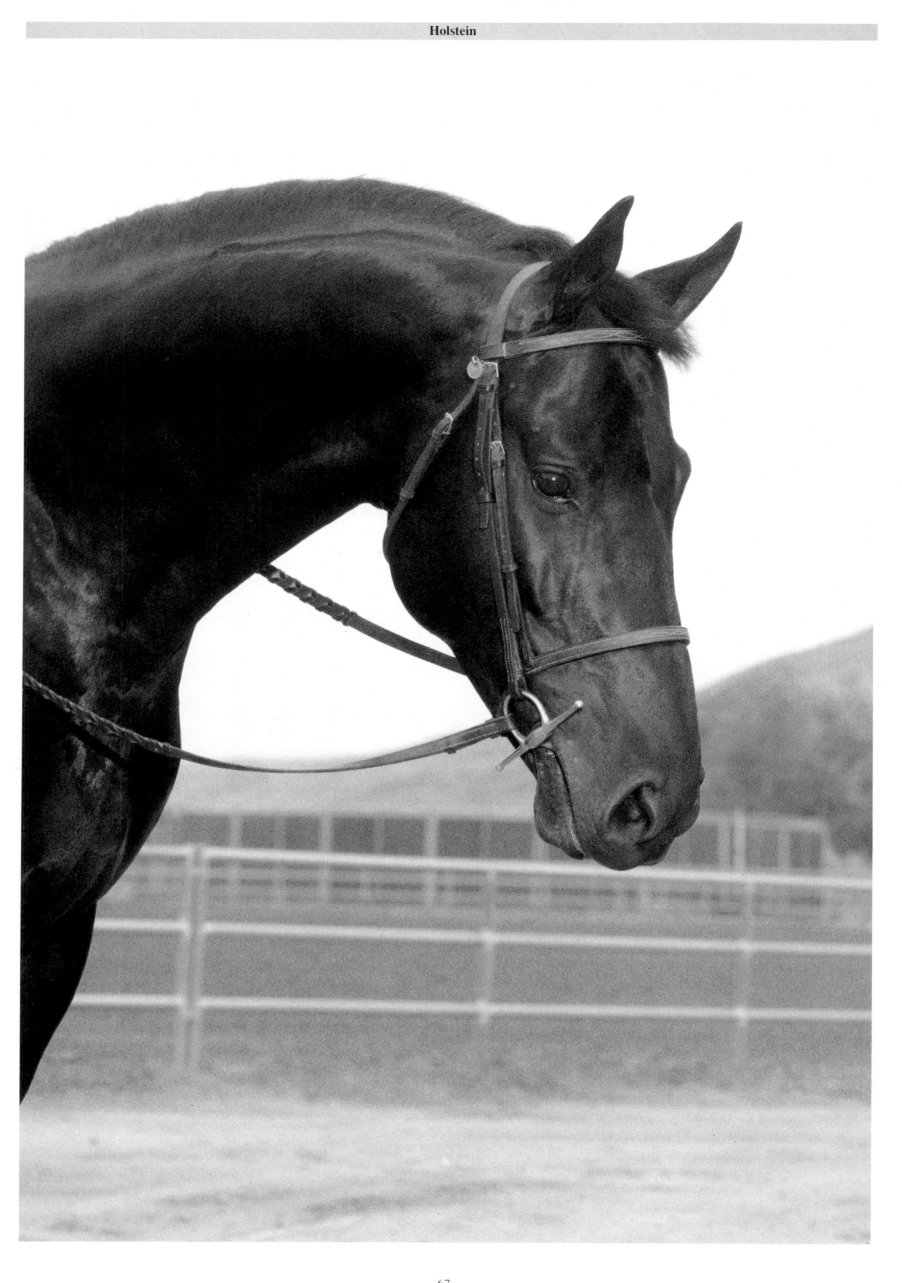

HUCUL

Native to the Carpathian Mountains of eastern Europe, the little (13 hand) dun-colored Hucul is related to the primitive Tarpan, itself a link to the ancient horses of the ice age. Influenced slightly by Arabian stock, the Hucul has been systematically bred in limited numbers since the nineteenth century.

ICELANDIC PONY

These ponies have adapted well to life in bleak, cold Iceland, high on the Arctic Circle between Norway and Greenland. They are descended from the horses that were imported to Iceland when the Norsemen settled there in 874. For the past 800 years, no horses or ponies have been imported to Iceland, so these native ponies are perhaps the purest in blood line of all breeds. Like the Shetland, they thrive with even the most modest care and feeding. Exceedingly strong and compact in build, these usually dun-colored ponies average 12 to 13 hands. They are the only five-gaited saddle horses in Europe. The five gaits are: the Walk, the Trot, the Canter, the Pace and the Running Walk. Few horses *ever* combine the latter two.

In 1959 and 1960, the Lee brothers of Alberta, Canada imported three stallions and about 670 mares. Later, George Williams of Boulder, Colorado imported mares and a stallion. Eventually, the Icelandic Pony Club & Registry was formed at Greeley, Colorado.

These pages: **Icelandic ponies — a friendly, docile and independent breed. They are extremely hardy and very talented saddle horses.**

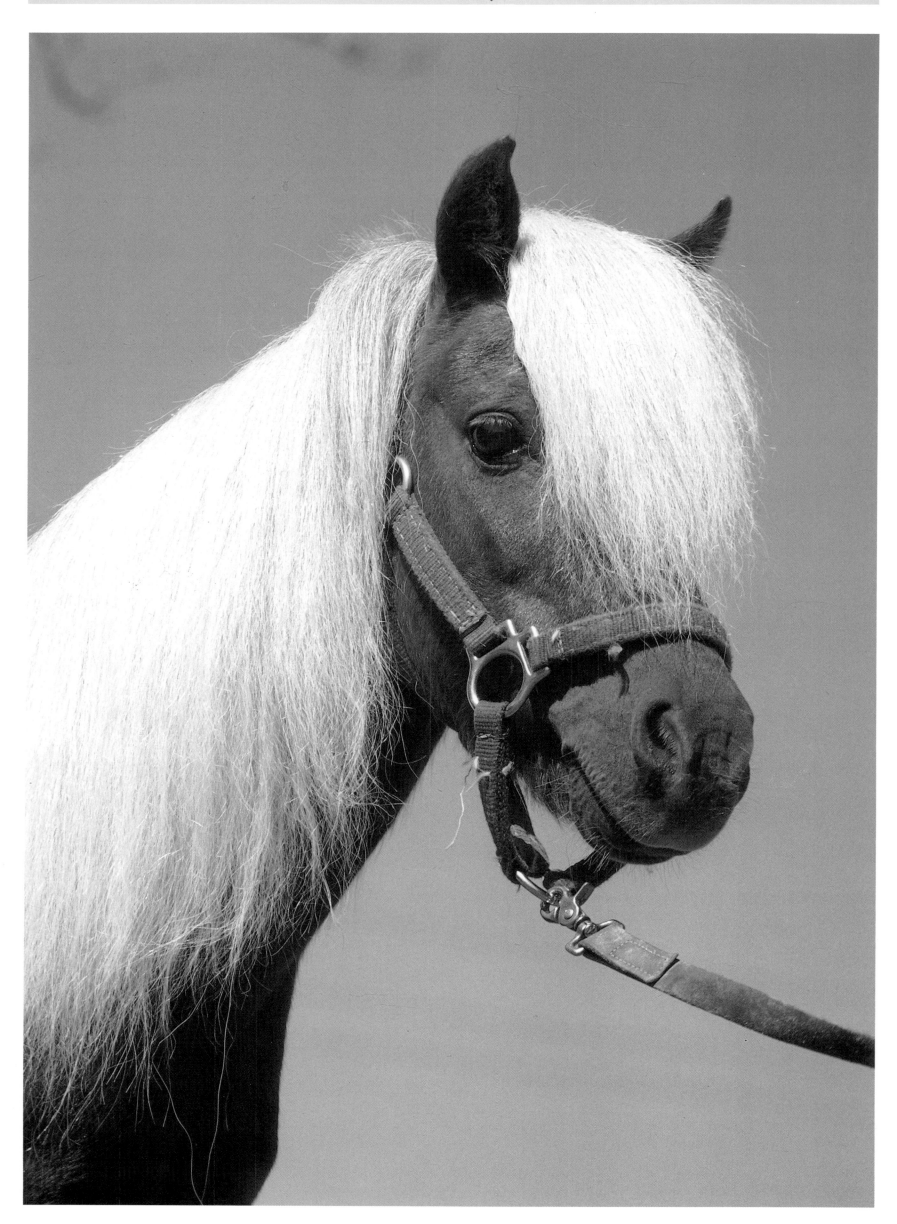

ILI (See MONGOLIAN)

INDONESIAN

The islands of the vast Indonesian archipelago of southeast Asia are home to a number of fairly distinct breeds, which we have chosen to combine here because they are obviously descended from a common ancestry and because their physical characteristics are roughly similar. The Indonesian breeds include the Bali (island of Bali), Batak (island of Sumatra), Java (island of Java), Sandalwood (islands of Sumba and Sumbawa), Sumba (island of Sumba), Sumbawa (island of Sumbawa), and the Timor (island of Timor).

These breeds each vary greatly in color, although the Bali, Sumba and Sumbawa are characterized by a black dorsal stripe. With the exception of the tiny Timor, which averages 9 to 11 hands, all the Indonesian types average between 12 and 13 hands. All the Indonesian breeds are used both for riding and draft work, and the Sandalwood is also used in organized local racing.

IOMUD

Closely related to the Turkoman and Akhal-Teké, the Iomud also originated in central Asia, specifically Turkestan (part of what is now the Soviet Union). The Iomud is typically grey, although it can be any color, and stands 14.2 to 15 hands. The most unique feature of this horse is its ability to withstand the extreme temperatures of the desert and to survive long periods of time without water. Among four-legged pack animals, only the camel can match or exceed the Iomud's ability to go without drinking for so long.

IRISH COB (See COB)

IRISH DRAFT

The name for this horse is somewhat misleading because it has now developed into a fabulous show and jumping horse. After the time of the great Irish Potato Famine, its usual appearance and build became even coarser due to the infusion of Shire and Clydesdale blood. Finally, by the turn of the century, the US Department of Agriculture introduced subsidies for the improvement of the breed in the United States.

In 1917 the stud book was started, and it currently lists about 8000 horses. In 1976 the Irish Draft Horse Society was formed, and three years later, in 1979, the English recognized the Irish Draft as a breed rather than a subtype, and the British-Irish Draft Horse Society was formed. This horse averages 16 hands and ranges from bay to chestnut in color.

IRISH HUNTER

This tall horse is bred as a hunting horse and as an exhibition jumper. It varies widely in color, and averages 16 hands in height.

ITALIAN HEAVY DRAFT

Originally developed during the middle nineteenth century in the Po River delta, this breed was influenced by various draft types, as well as by Thoroughbred and Hackney stock. Both Ardennes and Percheron blood entered the line in the twentieth century, and the stud book was officially established in 1961. This horse averages 15 to 16 hands and is typically dark chestnut, with a light mane and tail.

JAF

This breed originated in Iran, and is used today primarily as a saddle horse. It ranges in color from chestnut or grey, to brown or bay, and stands approximately 15 hands.

JAVA (See INDONESIAN)

JUTLAND

Native to northern Denmark, this breed originated in the early Middle Ages and was used by the Vikings, and later in jousting tournaments. In the nineteenth century the breed was influenced by the introduction of Suffolk and Cleveland Bay blood. The Jutland is used today primarily as a draft animal. This horse is usually chestnut, with a light mane and tail, and averages 15.3 hands in height.

KABARDIN

First bred by the Uzbeks of central Asia, this breed is used today primarily as a saddle horse, as a pack animal or under harness. The Kabardin is known for being particularly sure-footed in mountainous

Below: **The local blacksmith of Ennistymon, County Clare, Ireland, practices his trade for the upkeep of a customer's beautiful bay Irish Hunter.**

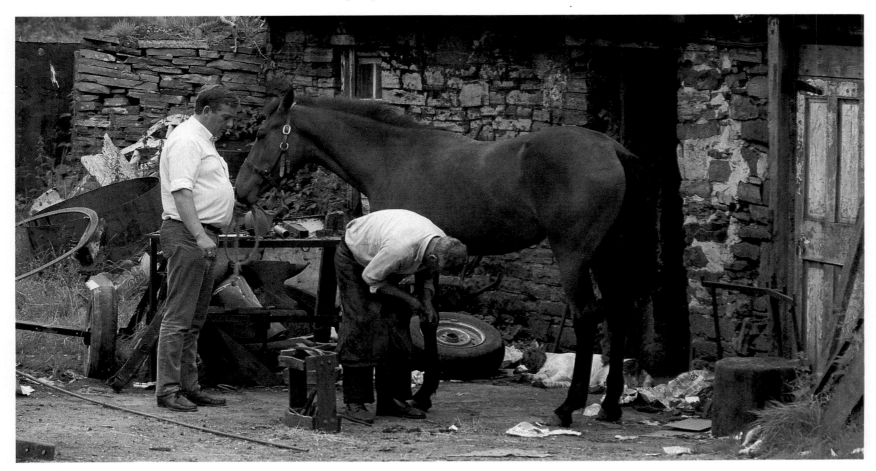

terrain. It is usually bay, dark bay or black in coloring and averages 15 hands in height.

KARABAIR

Today used as a saddle or light draft horse, the Karabair originated in the mountains of Russia and has been influenced over time by the influx of Arabian blood. In turn, this breed has influenced the development of the Don. The Karabair is usually grey or bay, and averages 15 hands in height.

KARABAKH

This breed originated in the Azerbaidzhan region of the Soviet Union and has a strong Oriental influence. It is used today primarily as a saddle and pack horse, is varied in color, and averages 14.1 hands in height.

KARACABEY

Originally bred in Turkey from Nonius stallions and local mixed-blood mares, the Karacabey is used as a saddle and pack horse. It ranges in height from 15.2 to 16.1 hands and in color from bay to black or grey.

KAZAKH

This pony from the steppes of central Asia traces its lineage to the wild horses of the region, with strong influence from the Don horse. The Kazakh is divided into two subtypes: the rugged and compact Dzhabe, and the sleeker, more gentle Adayev, which has been influenced by the Akhal-Teké and Karabair stock.

KHAYLAN (See ARABIAN)

KIRGHIZ (NOVOKIRGHIZ)

This horse evolved in central Asia in what is now the Soviet Republic of the same name, and was originally used by the nomads of the region. Since 1930 it has been greatly changed by crossbreeding with Don and Thoroughbred stock, with the result of the breed being officially renamed Novokirghiz ('new Kirghiz') in 1954. This breed is used primarily as a pack or saddle horse. It is dark in color and averages 15 hands in height.

KLADRUBER

With an average height of 16.2 to 17 hands, some examples of this enormous draft breed have been known to stand 18 hands, probably making it the largest in the world. It was first bred in 1572 at the royal stud farm at Kladruby in Bohemia by Emperor Maximillian II. The breed's two characteristic colors can be traced to two specific foundation sires: black to *Sacromoso* (1799) and grey to *Pepoli* (1764).

KNABSTRUP

This horse was derived in Denmark from Frederiksborg stock, and is used today primarily as a show horse, both under saddle and harness. It averages 15 hands in height. Originally a spotted horse, it no longer displays this characteristic — which established it as a separate breed from the Frederiksborg.

KONIK

This dun-colored, all-purpose breed originated in Poland, and is closely related to the primitive Tarpan. It has, in turn, been used for the development of many other breeds in both eastern Europe and the USSR. It averages 13.1 hands in height.

KURDISTAN

Originally from the Kurdish region of eastern Turkey, this breed is used today for many purposes, from saddle horse to draft animal. This horse varies in color, and averages 14 hands in height.

LANDAIS (BARTHAIS)

Native to southwestern France, the Landais is still found in a semi-wild state in the Adour River country, although fewer than 150 still remain. At the turn of the century, however, there were more than 2000. It is a small horse, 11.2 to 13 hands in height, and ranges in color from bay to black.

LIPIZZANER

The Lipizzaner horse was first bred in the forests of what was then part of the Austro-Hungarian Empire, but is now in northwestern

The exquisite Lipizzaners are among the world's most talented horses. *Below:* Lipizzaner carriage horses in Vienna. Lipizzaner colorings other than the typical gray are bay, chestnut and roan.

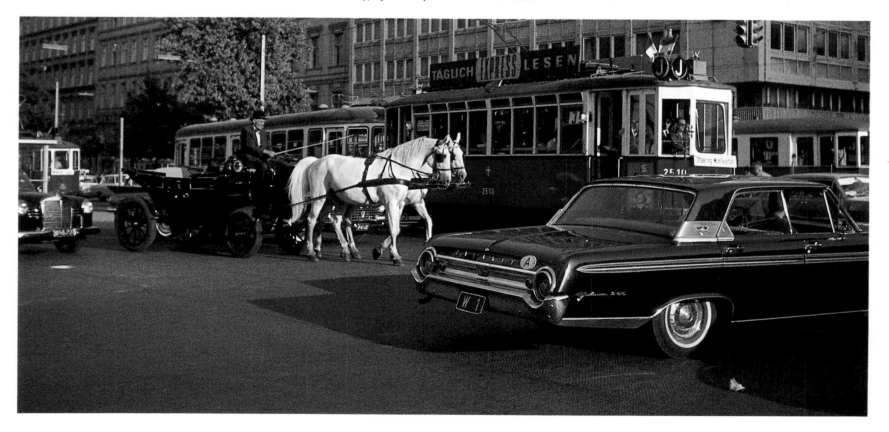

Yugoslavia, at the Lipica (Lipizza) estate. This breed is typically, though not exclusively, all white. Lipica covers over 700 acres. Today, more than 400 years later, despite desperate years of war and vast political changes, the Lipica estate has survived virtually intact.

At the height of the Austro-Hungarian Empire, Lipica supplied the horses for the Viennese Court and for the exclusive Spanish Riding School, which was established in Vienna by Emperor Charles VI in 1729. However, from the end of World War I until the end of World War II, activities at Lipica were dominated by the Italian military.

The Lipizzaner fate during the wars is fascinating. When Italy declared war on Austria in late May 1915, the herd was moved to Luxembourg. Unfortunately, the climate did not agree with the horses and this, coupled with poor quality hay, caused the death of 31 mares carrying foals. After the war, when the Italians took over the estate, General Carlo Petitti, then governor of Guilian province, appointed a commission to go to Vienna and negotiate with the Austrian government for the return of the Lipizzaners. After lengthy discussions, a compromise was reached which awarded 109 horses to Italy and 98 to Austria.

The Austrians then moved their herd to Piber near Graz and began breeding their own Lipizzaners. Today, these stables supply all the horses used by the Spanish Riding School. For three years, between 1927–1930, first Arabians and then Thoroughbred stallions were tried for crossbreeding, but the offspring were not suited to the climate, and the experiment was abandoned.

Near the end of World War II, when the Russian Red Army advanced toward Sudentenland in a last minute sweep, Colonel Podhajski, director of the Spanish Riding School in Vienna, grew concerned about the welfare of the Lipizzaners, because without them the School could not survive. In response to his urgent request, the American Third Army, under the command of General George M

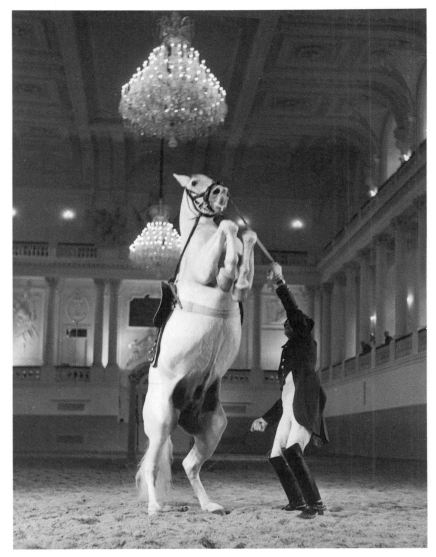

At right and below: **Lipizzaners in performance at the famous and historic Spanish Riding School in Vienna.** *At far right:* **A Lipizzaner with mottled coat.**

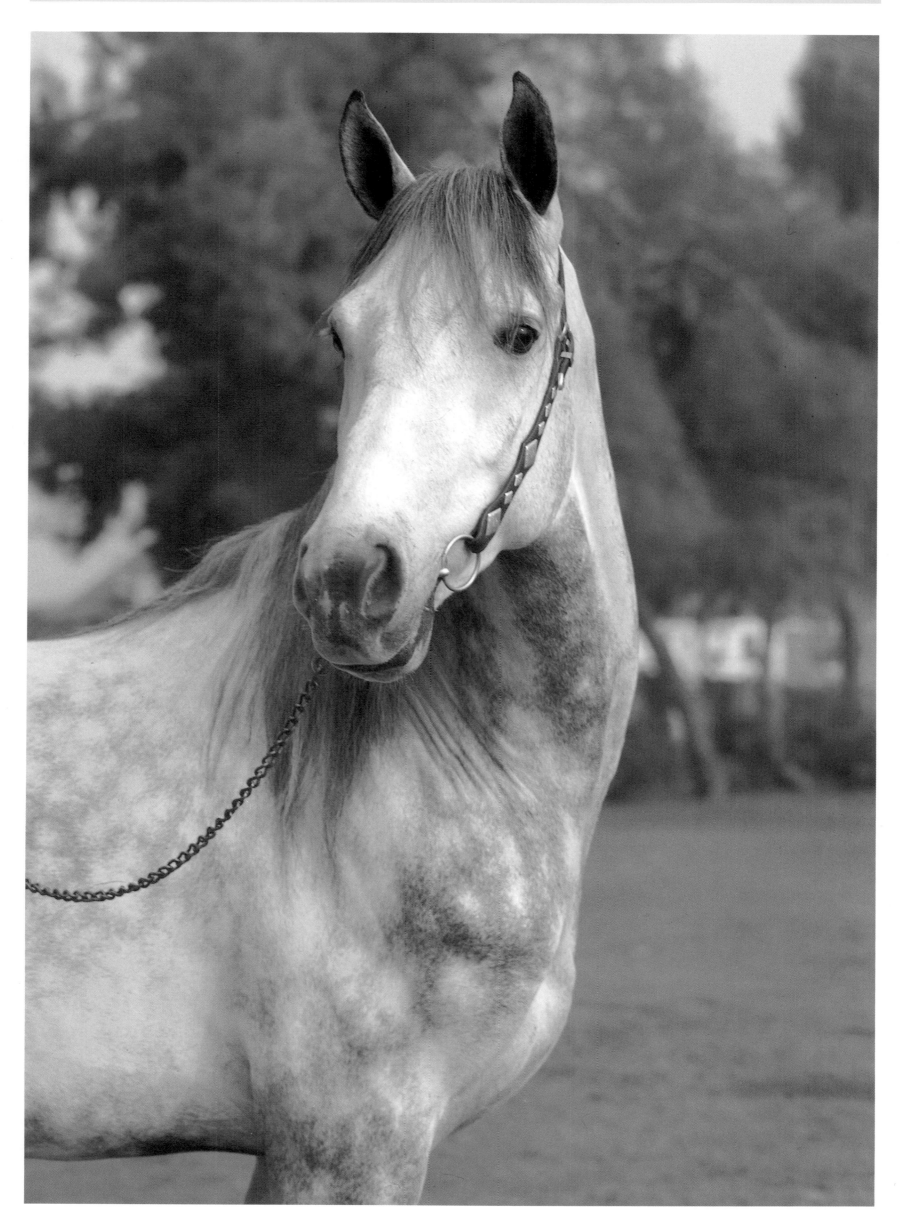

Patton, carried out a daring rescue of the stallions and guided them to Schwarzenberg in Bavaria.

Lipizzaner foals are born black or another dark color, but by the time they are a year old they already have a sprinkling of white hairs. They are known for their superior intelligence, proud bearing, beauty and strength, but most of all for their ability to execute graceful, precise dance maneuvers. Besides the various quadrilles, Lipizzaners perform half passes — both right and left — pirouettes, piaffes, passage levades, courlettes, ballotades, and caprioles, as well as trots and canters.

LATVIAN HARNESS HORSE (LITHUANIAN HEAVY DRAFT)

These two big breeds originated in the nineteenth century in the small Baltic nations of the same names, and are used today primarily as draft animals. Both the Latvians and Lithuanians are usually chestnut to bay in color and average 16 hands in height.

LLANERO (A Venezuelan form of CRIOLLO)

LOKAI

Related to the Karabair from which it is derived, this horse also shows a strong Arabian influence. The Lokai originally evolved during the sixteenth century in the mountains of what is today the Tadzhik Republic of the USSR. It ranges in color from chestnut to gray and usually stands 14.3 hands.

LUSITANO

The Portuguese Lusitano is similar in appearance to the Spanish Andalusian, and is a very intelligent and graceful animal. This breed is used for everyday riding and light farm work, but also for a more illustrious, but dangerous, duty: Portuguese bull fighting! In this sport, the bull is fought from horseback. It occurs in solid colors and averages 15.1 hands in height.

MANGALARGA (See CRIOLLO)

MANIPURI

The Manipuris evolved from horses introduced onto the subcontinent of India by the Tartars of the north around 700 AD. They were the original polo pony, having been the horse of choice when the game developed in India. When polo was adopted by the British in the nineteenth century, Manipuris were part of the package, and they are still used in the game today because of their native agility and quick acceleration. They range in color from bay to chestnut and stand 11 to 13 hands tall.

MARWARI

This horse was originally bred in India, and is used in the subcontinent today primarily as a saddle horse. The Marwari may be any color, or multicolored, and averages 14 hands in height. Another Indian pony, the Kathiawora, closely resembles this breed.

MASUREN

Originally bred in Poland, this solid-colored breed is used today for a wide spectrum of tasks, ranging from those of a draft horse to harness racing. It averages 16 hands in height.

MECKLENBURG

This breed originated in Germany, in the region of its namesake, and is used today primarily as a riding horse. It is currently bred under the control of the East German government. This horse is of solid color, and averages 16 hands in height.

MÉRENS (See ARIÈGEOIS)

At right: **This Lipizzaner shows a correct, natural stance.**

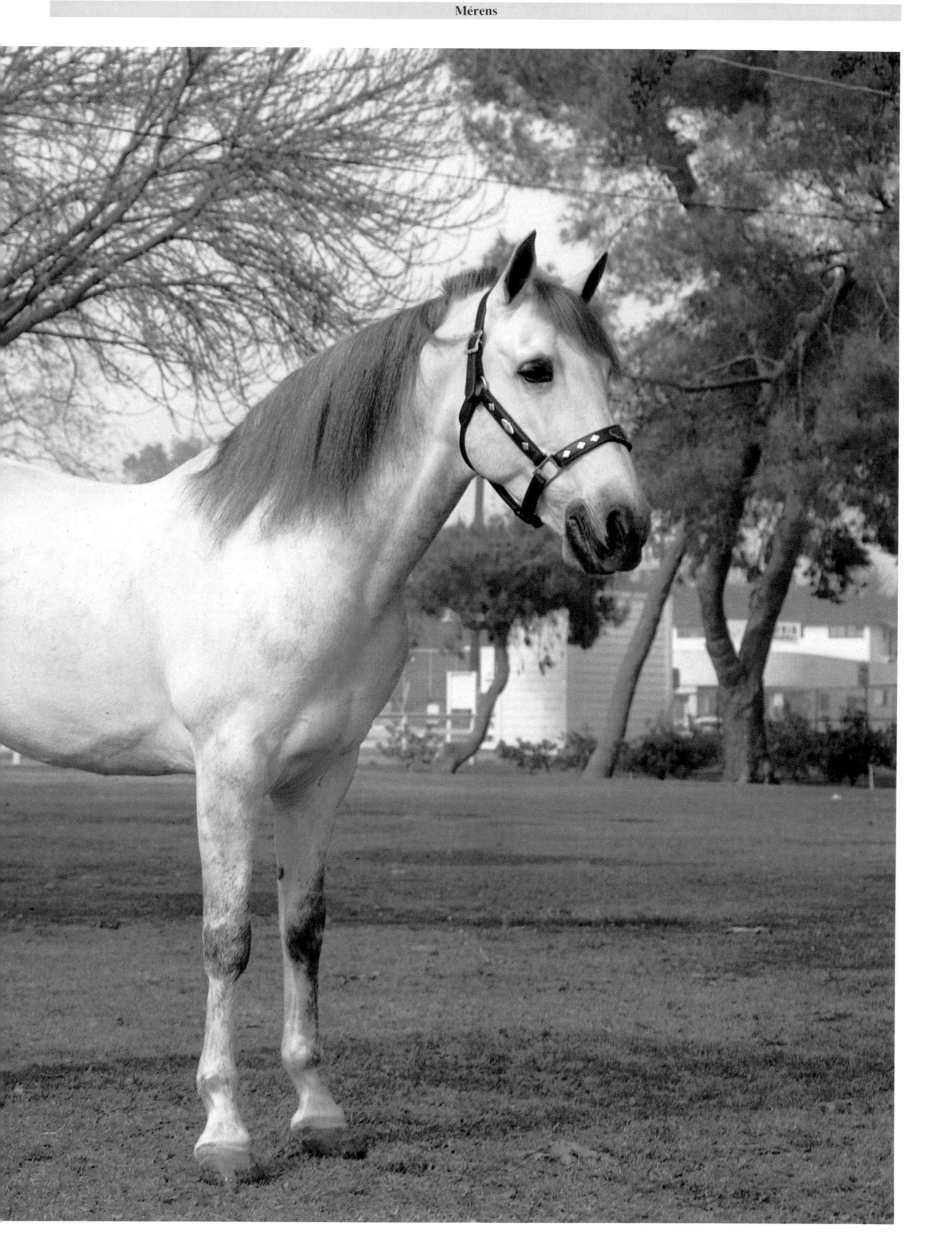

MÉTIS TROTTER

Native to the Soviet Union, this breed was developed in the early twentieth century by crossing Orlov Trotters with American Standard-bred horses, for competition with American and French trotting horses. Officially recognized since 1949, the breed is used today primarily for harness racing, and, as such, is also known as the Russian Trotter. This horse may be any color and averages 15.1 to 15.3 hands in height.

MIDGET HORSES

Midget horses have been bred in many parts of the world, but were always referred to as 'ponies.' Today, this has become a thriving business, and breeders no longer will allow their stock to be referred to as ponies. In fact, with careful, selective breeding, these miniature animals now appear more like a full-sized horse than a pony.

The family of Julio Cesar Falabella of Buenos Aires, Argentina are among the most well known breeders in the world and have given their name to a variety of midgets that are rarely taller than 7 hands. In 1962 the Falabellas sold some midgets to the Kennedy family, and the notoriety of this sale so increased business, that they soon had a herd of 400, the largest in the world. These little animals now bring at least $1500 for a gelding, $2000 for a mare, and $3000 for a stallion.

Smith McCoy of Raderfield, West Virginia has very fine breeding stock that consistently produces horses which average 32 inches or less, full grown. Mr McCoy's full grown *Sugardumpling* is only 5 hands (20 inches) tall and, as such, is rated as one of the tiniest horses in the world. Another horse, *Tom Thumb*, owned by Arch McAskill in Texas, stands 5.3 hands (23 inches) and weighs 45 lbs. His 'stablemate,' *Cactus*, boasts 6.2 hands (26 inches) and 95 lbs.

Below: A nun at the monastery of Saint Clare in Brenham, Texas with a Midget Horse in her arms. *At right:* A Midget Horse with an unusual mane. *Overleaf:* A very sturdy Midget Horse.

MINHO (See GARRANO)

MISSOURI FOX TROTTER

Whereas some horses are registered on the basis of size or color, this animal is registered on the basis of its four-beat (foxtrot) gait. This characteristic — and clearly audible rhythm — is produced by the animal cantering with its forelegs and trotting or walking with its hind legs. The Missouri Fox Trotter is a durable and very desirable saddle horse. Its color may vary widely, from bay to black or grey, and it typically measures 14 to 16 hands.

At right: A registered Missouri Foxtrotter, *Zane's Esther Bunny*, owned by Anita Rolfe. *Below:* Missouri Foxtrotters, a white and a sorrel chestnut. *At far right:* A bay Missouri Foxtrotter with a striped face, white muzzle and forehead star. *Overleaf:* A beautiful sorrel chestnut Missouri Foxtrotter displays the grace inherent in quality horses of this outstanding breed.

MORGAN

The foundation of the Morgan breed is unique in that it traces back to a single horse. The Morgan is the only breed that is named after a singing master, as well as being the oldest distinct breed in America. Justin Morgan was a frail Vermont music teacher and composer of hymns who owned a little horse, today referred to either as 'Justin Morgan's Horse,' or simply as *Justin Morgan*. Foaled in 1789 and died in 1821, this animal is said to have weighed no more than 850 pounds and to have stood 14 hands. However, in log pulling contests he bested the strongest horses in the surrounding area—most of them 400 pounds heavier than he! Morgan's horse was also entered in many quarter-mile races against the swiftest horses that could be found. There, too, he won every time. As a stallion—because of the foresight of his owner—he was mated with the best mares, and his prepotency was so great that he was able to pass on his remarkable speed, strength, endurance and his wonderfully gentle disposition to his progeny.

At right: **A chestnut Morgan mare and her foal in a frolicsome run.** *Below and at bottom:* **Morgans of the Morgan Horse Ranch, at Point Reyes National Seashore, California.** *Overleaf:* **Morgans grazing at the Morgan Horse Ranch.**

There are, of course, many differences of opinion as to the ancestry of Justin Morgan's little horse. Some researchers have said that his sire was a Dutch bred stallion. Others claim to have 'found' that his sire was a horse named *True Briton*. Here, too, there is disagreement. Some say that *True Briton* was a Thoroughbred, while others say that he was a Welsh Cob, and still others are sure that he was an Arabian. Those that have seen the statue of the little horse at the Morgan Horse Farm in Vermont can attest to the fact that the horse leans strongly to the Cob in appearance and conformation.

About 1870, Col Battell of Middleford, Vermont began gathering information about the Morgan Horse, and continued until his death in 1915. Interest in the history of the Morgan Horse was kept alive by the US Department of Agriculture. In 1907, Col Battell donated 400 acres near Middleford, Vermont to the US Department of Agriculture for use as a Morgan horse farm, and the present location of the American Morgan Horse Association, Inc is in Shelburne, Vermont. The National Park Service also has a small Morgan farm at Point Reyes, California.

The description of the dam of *Justin Morgan*, given on page 95 of Volume I of the Morgan Horse Register, is as follows: 'The dam of the Morgan horse was of the Wild Air or Wildair breed; she was of middling size, her color was a light bay, mane and tail not dark, hair on legs rather long; she was a smooth, handsome traveler. Her sire was the Diamond, a thick, heavy horse of middle size; he had a thick, bushy mane and tail; a smooth traveler.'

At right: **A Morgan colt with a forehead star.** *Below:* **A National Park Service ranger and a chestnut Morgan.** *At far right:* **A bay Morgan with a star and stripe.**

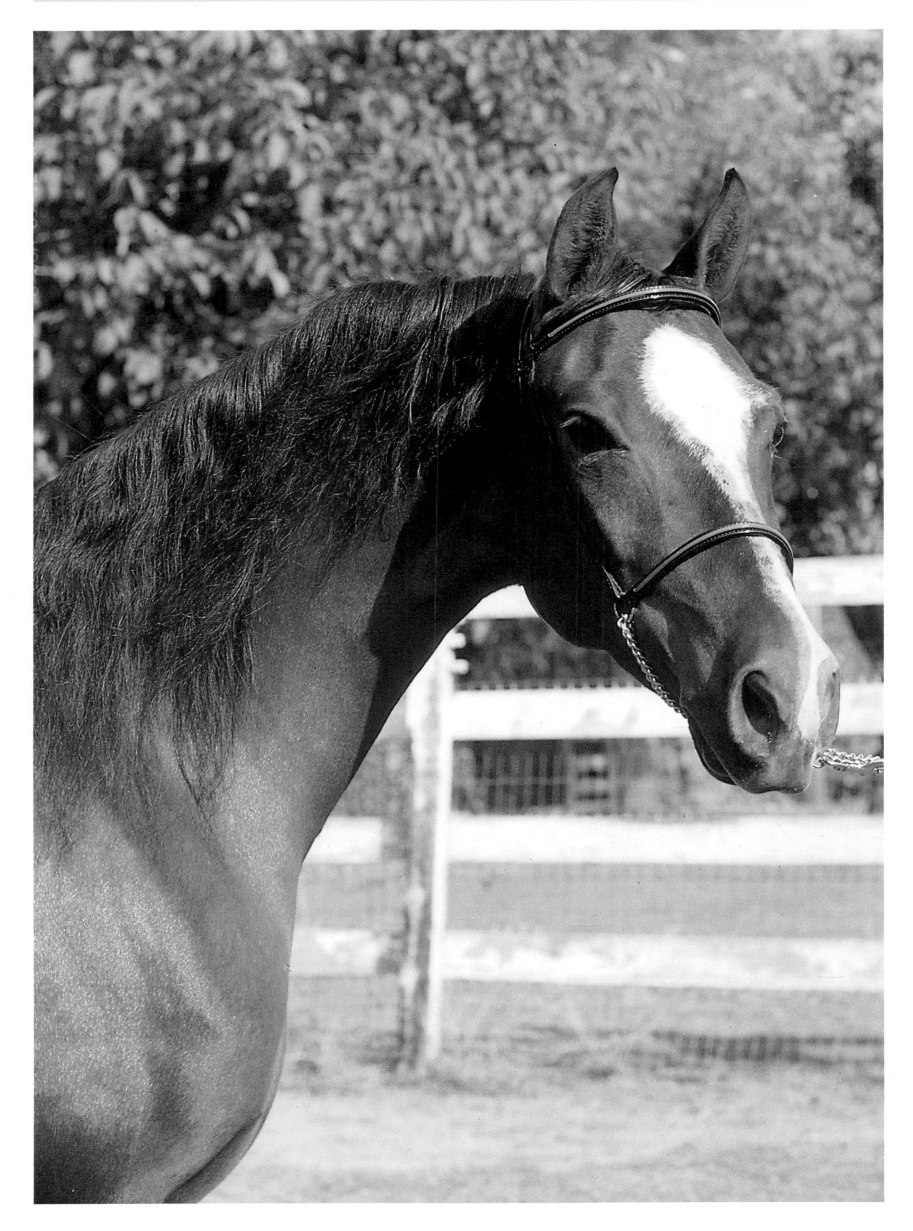

Dr CD Parks, having extensively researched Justin Morgan's Horse's pedigree, concludes that: 'It is reasonable to believe that the dam of *Justin Morgan* was three-quarters Dutch and one-quarter grade Arabian. *Justin Morgan* would then be five-eighths grade Arabian and three-eighths Dutch. He had the bay color, heavy black mane and tail and long hair about the fetlocks, which belonged to the Dutch horse. The horses, so far as we can determine, native to the section of Vermont where *Justin Morgan* produced most of his offspring, were essentially the same as those credited with producing him.'

The way that *Justin Morgan*'s blood was perpetuated is clearly described in the Morgan Horse Register. The dam of *Sherman*, given on page 132 of Volume I of the Morgan Horse Register, is as follows: 'She was a chestnut, of good size, high spirited and an elegant animal. We called her of Spanish breed.' This would indicate that she was a grade Arabian. The dam of *Bulrush*, described on page 149 of Volume I of the Register, is as follows: 'She was a dark bay, with black legs, and heavy mane and tail; she was low and compact,

Below: **A rider on a chestnut Morgan at the Morgan Horse Ranch in California.** *At bottom:* **Note the shape of this Morgan's head.** *At right:* **A Morgan and foal.**

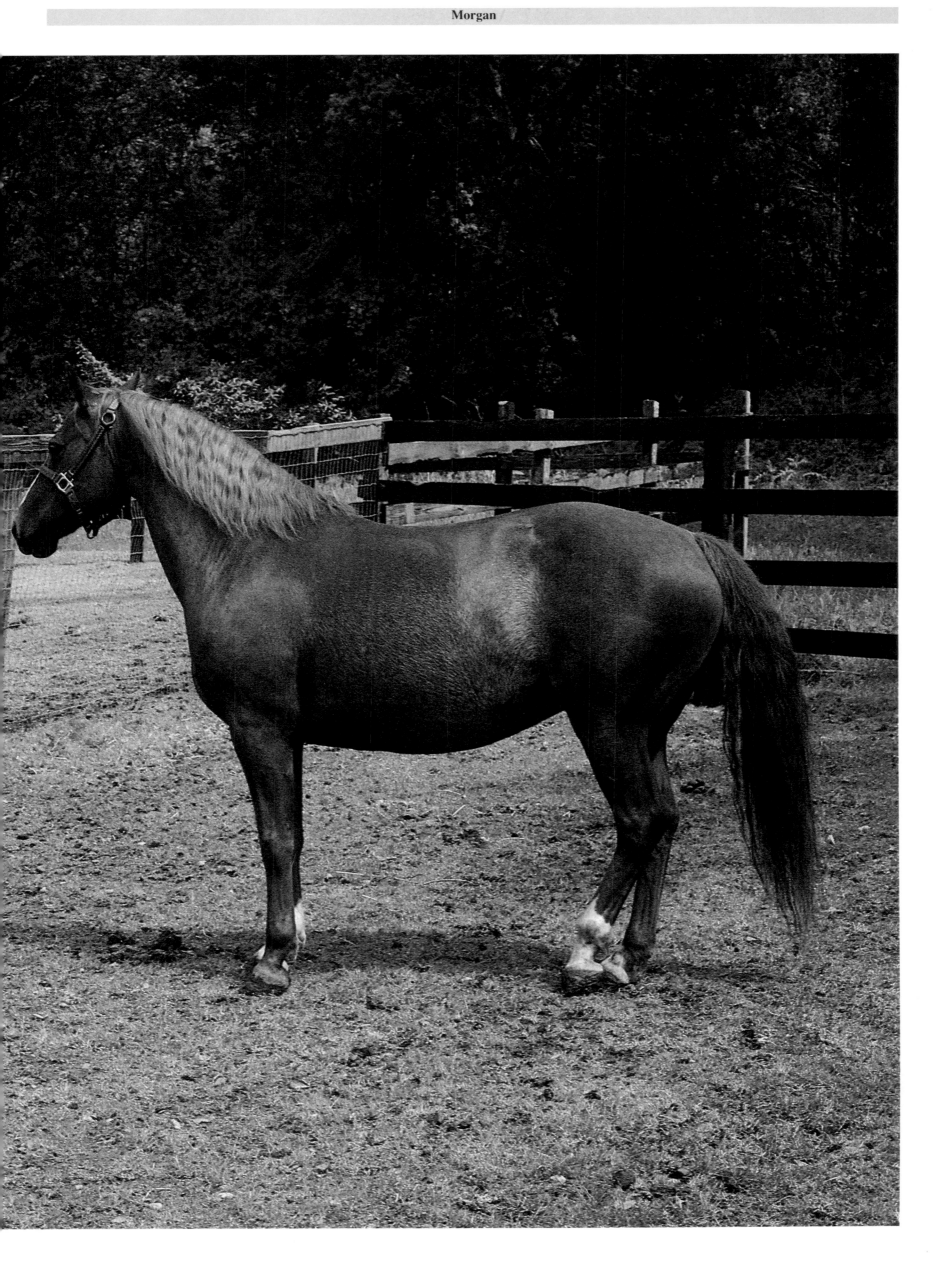

had heavy limbs, with large joints, neck rather long, a good head, but did not carry it up well; she was a sharp trotter, but was not a very spirited driver; she was said to be, and had the appearance of being, part French.'

For many years, in each succeeding generation, the blood of the Morgan was diluted. Experts consider it very unusual that through all of this, his descendants continue to inherit his characteristics, spirit, shape and intelligence so closely. Their step is short, nervous and energetic. Their great endurance rivals that of the Arabian, and they are used primarily for English and Western riding, as well as driving, like the great Morgan jumper ridden by General Humberto Mariles, which won a gold medal at the London Olympics in 1948. Indeed, today's Morgan can be enjoyed as a pleasure horse, a working cowboy's horse, or a show horse. Many are crossbred successfully with other breeds to make quarter-mile running horses or harness horses for racing, pleasure or show.

At right: **A Morgan foal at the Morgan Horse Ranch.** *Below:* **A very beautiful chestnut Morgan. Note its flaxen mane and tail.** *At far right:* **A Morgan foal with stripe, star and white muzzle.** *Overleaf:* **Morgans in the California surf.**

MONGOLIAN

Related to the Chinese Horse, this breed also originated in the steppes and deserts of central Asia, and served Ghenghis Kan and his hordes on their forays into the west. These horses, in turn, have made their influence felt on a great many other breeds throughout Eurasia. They are still used today by the nomadic people of central Asia for a variety of purposes. These horses are slightly larger than the Chinese horse, averaging 13 hands in height. Important subtypes include the Ili, Wuchumutsin, Hailar, Sanho, Sanpeitze and Heilung Chiang.

MONGOLIAN WILD HORSE

(See PRZEWALSKI'S HORSE)

MOROCHUCO

Originally bred in Peru, this breed is used today primarily as a saddle horse. This horse is a sub-type of the Salteño, the Peruvian name for the Criollo.

MOUNTAIN (See WELSH MOUNTAIN)

MUNIGHI (See ARABIAN)

MURAKOZ

Developed in the Mura River country of Hungary, this big animal is a typical 16 hand European draft horse, with Ardennes and Percheron heritage. It may vary in color, but is usually chestnut with a light mane, tail and feathering on its legs.

MURGESE

Bred in the Puglia region of Italy while it was under Spanish rule, this horse still shows the influence of the Barb and Arab stallions that helped found the breed. In turn, the Murgese helped to influence development of the Lipizzaner, via the stallions exported to the Austrian court in 1874. The original Murgese stud farm was located at Foggia, and it was there in 1948 that the current breeders' association was formed. This horse is black, grey with a black head or, occasionally, bay or chestnut in color, and stands 15 hands tall.

MUSTANG

Descended from the horses brought to North America by the Spanish Conquistadors in the sixteenth century, the Mustang, or Spanish Mustang, takes its name from the Spanish *Mesteño*, which essentially means 'belonging to the horse raiser.' The *Mesteño* is, in turn, of Barb and Arabian ancestry and descended from the great war horses brought to the Iberian peninsula by the Moors in the eighth century.

According to the records of the American Mustang Association: 'The registration requirements of the different Spanish (speaking) countries were compared with each other, then compared with that which was determined about the Spanish horses at the time of the Conquistadors. This was then compared with the work of our own American writers, artists, and personal observation. Not unexpectedly, all the sources of information agreed. Yes, the Spanish descriptions of their stock were in agreement with the requirements of the South American associations. In turn, South American requirements were the same as those characteristics described by American writers. This data is the basis for the conformation standards of the American Mustang Association. The characteristics of an American Mustang

Below: **Southwest Spanish Mustang Association-registered Mustang mares, owned by Gilbert Jones of Oklahoma.** *At right:* **A Uinta Ute warrior and his new bride, on Mustangs tamed by their tribe, in 1874.**

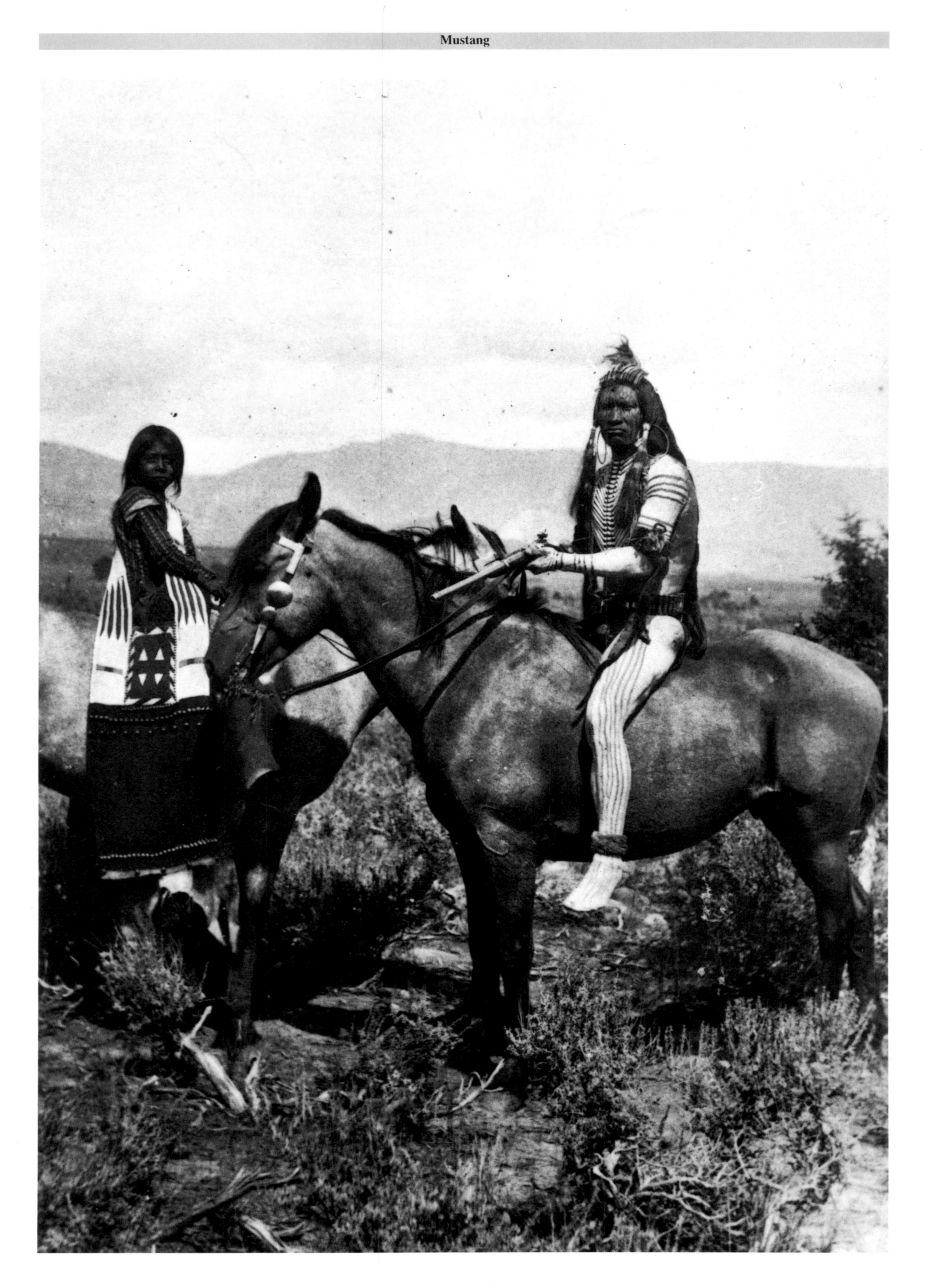

are as follows: the height is between 13.2 and 15 hands and the weight is usually between 700 and 1000 pounds; the build is compact, well proportioned, smooth muscled, and symmetrical; in conformation the back is short coupled, there is broad width between alert eyes, and moderate head length; the legs have good flexion, are straight, and have small to medium sized chestnuts; there is good slope to the shoulder, a deep crested neck which is shorter than most breeds', and moderate withers blending into the back; the chest is of moderate width, the rib cage is well sprung, and the barrel is deep; the hindquarters are strong, the croup is rounded, and the tail set is low; the horse shows great agility and power, is well balanced, and moves with the hindquarters well under the body weight; the American Mustang is long on endurance and intelligence and has a good, adaptable disposition. Coat color and marking patterns are varied; a Mustang may be any color, from solid to mixed combinations.'

Today's American Mustang is descended from horses that were either stolen from the Conquistadors by the Indians or escaped into the wild. By the nineteenth century, large herds of wild horses roamed the West, and it is a testament to the hardiness of this little breed that they survived. Wild herds still exist in Nevada, Oregon and the Pryor Mountains of Montana, but many Mustangs have been domesticated, and the breed has a large following. Several organizations have been established around the breed, with the Southwest Spanish Mustang Association of Finley, Oklahoma having been one of the first and still one of the most active. The American Mustang Association, founded in Yucaipa, California in 1962, boasts a membership in excess of one thousand, and holds an annual National Grand Championship Horse Show.

NEW FOREST PONY

Today approximately 2000 of these small, docile ponies wander semi-wild in the heather bogs and pastures of the New Forest in Hampshire, England. They were there when the New Forest became a hunting reserve for William the Conqueror in 1079, and they remain today. The New Forest commoners who own them also possess ancient grazing rights there.

Each autumn the New Forest 'agisters,' who are responsible for the welfare of the ponies, organize a 'drift,' or roundup. On the appointed day agisters mounted on fast ponies and accompanied by the commoners of that area herd the ponies into pounds, or railed enclosures. Here they worm them and cut their tails in a pattern designed to show that their grazing fees have been paid. Foals to be sold are cut out of the herd, and the remaining horses are turned back into the pasture.

Although extensively crossbred, particularly with the Dartmoor and other pony breeds, the New Forest Pony has clearly defined characteristics. As a result, it may be any color and ranges in height from 12.2 to 14.2 hands.

NIEDERSACHSEN (See RHINELAND)

NIGERIAN

This all-purpose breed originated in West Africa from Barb and Arabian stock brought in from North Africa in ancient times. It is smaller and more compact than its northern cousins, averaging 14.1 hands in height.

Below: **Young Southwest Spanish Mustang Association-registered mares raised on Medicine Spring Ranch, near Finley, Oklahoma.**

NONIUS

This breed is descended from cavalry horses captured by the Austrians after Napoleon's defeat in the Battle of Leipzig. Today these animals are bred at Mezöhegyes farm in Hungary and are used both in harness racing and as saddle horses. They are usually found in dark, solid colors, and average 14.2 to 16.2 hands in height.

NORAM

Native to France, this horse is used today primarily as a racing trotter. This solid-colored breed averages 15.2 hands in height.

NORIC, or NORIKER

Frequently called the South German Cold-Blood, this breed originated in Bavaria and was influenced by horses brought north by the Romans. With later Andalusian influence, the breed was refined in the nineteenth century, although the stud book was not established until 1903. It is used today primarily as a draft and pack animal. Typically bay to brown or black, it averages 15.1 hands in height. The Pinzgainer breed, often considered a subtype of the Noric, is characterized by spots.

NORMAN (See SELLE FRANÇAIS)

NORMAN TROTTER

(See FRENCH TROTTING HORSE)

NORTH SWEDISH

As the name implies, this horse originated in northern Sweden, adjacent to Lapland, where the breed registry was established in 1924. Today this breed is used both as a draft horse and as a racing trotter. It is bay or brown, and averages 15.2 hands in height.

NORTHLANDS

This all-purpose breed originally evolved in the Baltic region from wild Tarpan and Mongolian stock. Usually dark-colored, it averages 13 hands in height.

NORWEGIAN (See FJORD PONY)

NUMIDIAN (See BARB)

OBERLANDER

This large breed originated in Germany, and is used today primarily as a pack or draft horse. This horse ranges from bay to brown and may often be spotted, and averages 15.1 hands in height. It is a lighter variant of the Noriker.

OBVINSKI (See VIATKA)

OLD ENGLISH HEAVY HORSE

(See SHIRE)

Below left, and right bottom: At the American Mustang Association National Grand Championship Horse Show. *Below right:* A Grand Champion.

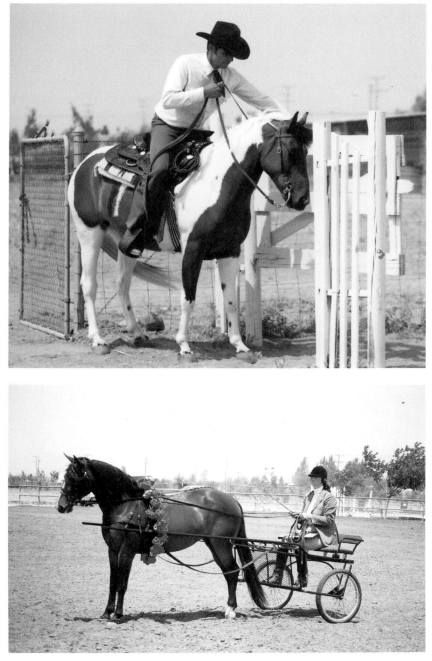

OLDENBURG

The Oldenburg is a very large horse, standing 16.2 to 17 hands or more. In color it varies from brown or bay to black, with the Rottaler branch of Bavaria almost always chestnut. Founded by Count Anton Gunther (1603–1667), this breed, like so many others, was cross-bred with Spanish Barb and English Thoroughbred. Today many titled families in Germany and England own Oldenburgs and use them as carriage and saddle horses.

ONAGER

Perhaps one of the first breeds to be used by mankind, this now extinct breed was domesticated by the Sumerians about 2000 BC. Onager stud farms once existed near the Black and Aral Seas and on the Tigris River. The horses were yoked to heavy four-wheeled carts and controlled by means of reins attached to nose rings.

ORLOV TROTTER

The Orlov was developed by Count Alexi Orlov in Imperial Russia in 1777 as a trotting horse. The foundation sire was *Smetanka*. Later, Arabian and Thoroughbred blood was introduced to improve the line. Today it is bred for harness and saddle, as well as for trotting races. This breed is usually grey or black, and averages 15.3 to 17 hands in height.

OVERO (See PINTO)

PAINT (See PINTO)

PALOMINO

In the early part of this century horsemen of the western United States began to notice — and greatly admire — foals with cream or golden yellow coloring and a very light colored mane and tail. No matter what breed of horse — whether Thoroughbred, Standardbred, Morgan, Arabian, Tennessee Walking Horse, or American Quarter

Below : **A nine-year-old Palomino stallion and owner Gay Cole of Cumberland, Maryland.** *At right and bottom:* **Palominos the color of a 'newly-minted penny.'**

Horse—owners started mating these beautiful horses with another with the same coloring. At first, no thought was given to pedigree, just to appearance. Indeed, the distinctive 'palomino color' is common to a great many other breeds.

Color, rather than size, is the most important characteristic in determining members of the breed, although Palominos typically range between 14 and 15 hands. The genetics of the palomino coloring are not definitely known. Even today, there is no absolute guarantee that the foal of two Palominos will be of palomino color, even thought the color may have been constant on both sides for generations. The Palomino Horse Breeders Association of America was established in 1941 by Texas and California Palomino breeders, and has maintained a breeders' file to secure data on the breeding performances of stallions, with the hope that they can document the exact inheritance of the color pattern.

The four chief PHBA requirements for the registration of Palominos are:

1. No horse can be registered unless it is a Palomino and of a color pattern within the prescribed limits.
2. No horse can be registered if its sire or dam is a draft horse or a pony, or if the sire or dam is spotted or albino.
3. Sires or mares are not eligible for registration unless their sires and dams have been registered in the Palomino Horse Breeders of America, or in the registry of a recognized breed such as Thoroughbred, Arabian, Morgan, American Saddle Horse, Tennessee Walker, Quarter Horse, etc.
4. To be registered, all horses must be passed by a qualified and approved inspector of the Association. Geldings are eligible for registration on color alone.

The desired color of the Palomino is said to be that of a 'newly minted gold coin.' It can, of course, be a couple of shades darker or lighter and still be acceptable. Black hairs in the coats of Palominos, however, are considered undesirable. The mane and tail can be white, ivory or silver, with no more than 15 percent dark or chestnut hairs in either. The skin around the eyes must be dark, as must the eyes. Legs cannot have white above the knees or hocks and no white spots on the body are allowed. White markings on the face are permitted.

Below: Skipa Sweet Lady, **a winning mare at the World Champion Palomino Show.** *At right:* **A Palomino in a herd.** *Overleaf:* **Palominos in formation.**

PASO, PERUVIAN (See CRIOLLO)

PECHORA (See ZEMAITUKA)

PENEIA

This diminutive draft breed originated in the Peloponnesian region of Greece, and is still used today as a pack animal on the steep, narrow trails that cross the Balkan mountain ranges. It may be any color, and averages 12.1 hands in height.

PERCHERON (TRAIN PERCHERON)

Native to France, the Percheron derives its name from its native district of La Perche in Normandy. As with other draft breeds, the Percheron contains Flemish blood, but is trimmer in build because of early crosses with the Arabian. This trimness gives its head a more handsome appearance than the other draft breeds'.

Though most Percherons are born black, most later become dappled grey. At about 16 hands, its height is about the same as that of the Suffolk, but somewhat less than that of the Shire or Clydesdale. Averaging about 1800 pounds, it is generally lighter than the other major draft breeds.

In the United States and in the farm lands of South America the Percheron is the most popular of the draft breeds. Before the era of the railroads, stagecoaches used this breed because of its hard limbs and agile movement, as much as for its ability to maintain a steady trot tirelessly over long distances.

The original stud book was established at Nogent-le-Rotou in France in 1883, and a British society was founded in 1911. Percherons were always very popular in England and, indeed, during the nineteenth century they were used almost exclusively by the City of London for pulling omnibuses.

Beginning in 1902 there were various Percheron registries established in the United States under several names, eventually merging into the Percheron Horse Association of America.

Today there are over 250,000 Percherons registered in the United States but, as with other draft breeds, mechanization brought a sharp decline in interest in Percherons and a corresponding decline in their numbers.

PERSANO (See SALERNO)

PERUVIAN PASO/PERUVIAN STEPPING HORSE (See CRIOLLO)

PINDOS

This breed originated in the Thessalonika region of Greece, and is used today primarily as a pack animal and for the breeding of mules. These horses are typically bay, black or grey, and average 12.2 hands in height.

PINTO (also known as PAINT)

Webster's dictionary defines the Pinto as being 'a horse with irregular markings or spots.' This was the way the term was informally applied prior to 1963, when the Pinto (Paint) was officially recognized as a specific breed by the American Paint Horse Association.

Horses of broken or spotted color were depicted in drawings found on the walls of ancient European caves dating back to the fifteenth century BC. Records of the first domesticated horses contain drawings and paintings of spotted horses. According to Sam Savitt in

continued on page 110

Below: **Percherons in harness; they are included among the world's finest heavy horses.** *At right:* **A Pinto foal in a corral.** *Overleaf:* **Pintos at pasture.**

continued from page 106

his book, *American Horse*, Cortez brought two spotted stallions of Spanish Barb stock to America in 1519, and these are thought to have been responsible for the establishment of the breed in North America. Since then, there have always been a scattering of spotted horses among the bands of wild horses that roam the western plains, a fact which supports the contention that the spotted horse has been in North America for centuries. Always a favorite of the American Indian because of its beauty and natural camouflage pattern, the Pinto is also popular at major rodeos as a grand entry mount.

Spotting in animals is the result of inheritance for both color and spotting. In Pinto horses, there are two different basic color patterns. Naturally, there are countless variations of either pattern. Of the two basic patterns, the Tobiano has the larger, more boldly outlined spots with distinct borders. It is often described as a white horse with smooth-edged spots, or vice versa, a dark background with white spots. The Overo pattern, on the other hand, has finer, lacy-edged patterns and the spotting is more jagged along the edges. Overos also have more color along the backbone and on the legs. Many people would describe the Overo as a solid-colored horse with white decorations.

Below: A Tobiano Pinto at rest: note its large, smooth spots. *At bottom:* A fine Tobiano Pinto. *At right:* An Overo Pinto: note its small, irregular spots.

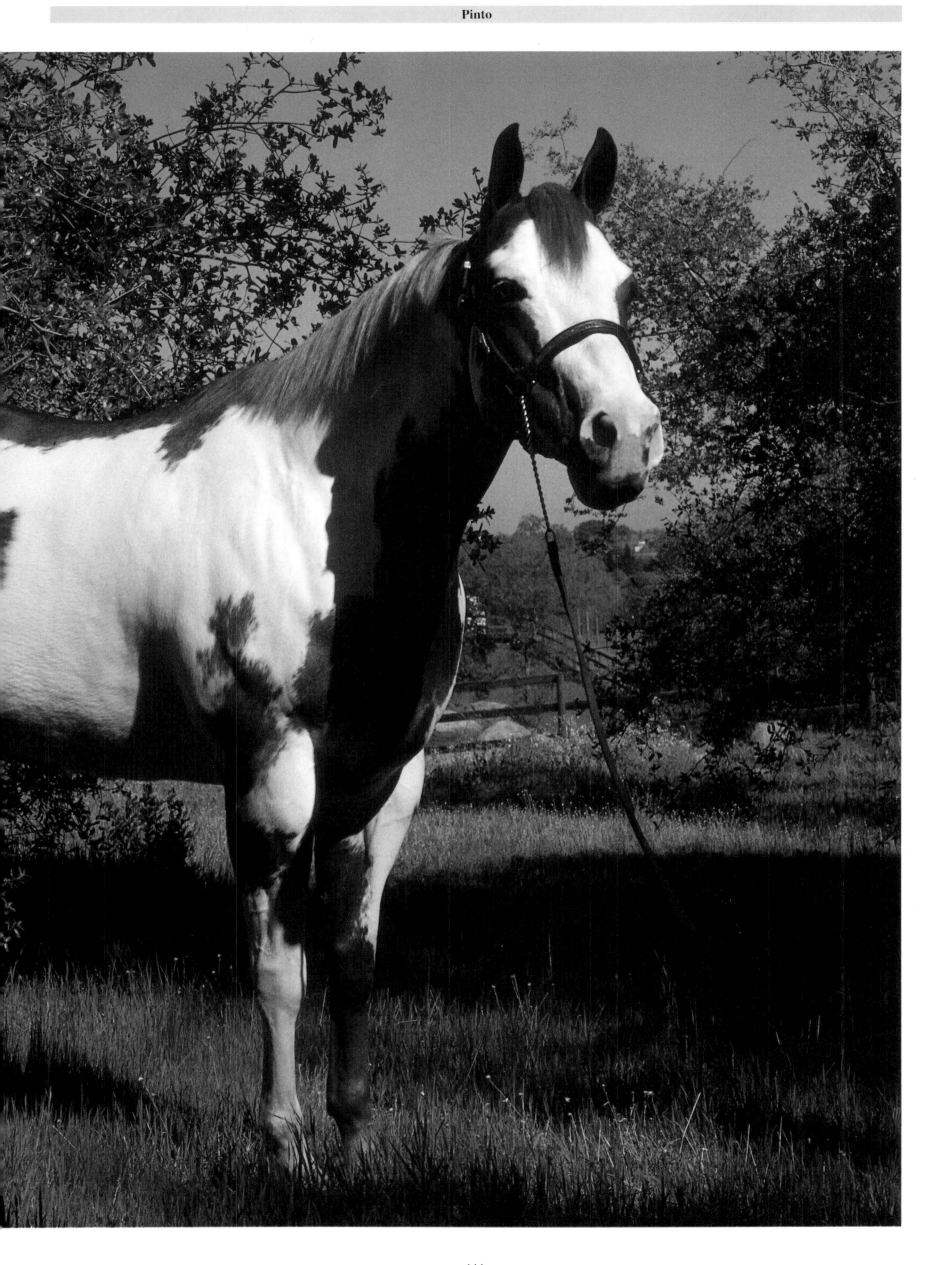

In registering Overo types, owners must be certain that their horses do not show Appaloosa characteristics, as the coloring of the Overo and Appaloosa are often quite similar. Breeders try to hold to an equal ratio of dark to light. Therefore, if a mare is more than half white, and a desirable dam, she is bred to a darker stallion.

Genetically, the Tobiano pattern appears to be the dominant one. If a Tobiano mare is bred to a Tobiano stallion, the chances are three to one that the foal will be spotted. If a solid-colored mare is bred to a Tobiano stallion, there is a an equal chance that the foal will either be spotted or solid in color. In breeding, conformation is always considered an important factor. Close inbreeding, however, is likely to produce animals of poor vitality, and crossing Pintos with grey or palomino color animals usually produces an animal with less desirable coloring. Thus, it is considered good policy to mate Tobiano to Tobiano and Overo to Overo to maintain top quality foals. Pintos range in size from 14.3 to 15.3 hands.

At right: An Overo Pinto at a gallop. *Below:* A beautiful Tobiano Pinto stallion. *At far right:* Two Pintos at pasture. *Overleaf:* Nearly solid-color Pinto mare and foal. The American Paint Horse Association is a proponent of the breed.

PINZGAUER

This breed originated in Austria and is thought by some to be a subtype of the closely related Noric. It is used today primarily as a draft or pack animal, and averages 15.3 hands in height. This horse ranges from bay to chestnut, and is often spotted, a characteristic which distinguishes it from the Noric.

PLEVEN (DANUBIAN)

First developed in the Georgi Dimitrov agricultural establishment near Pleven in Bulgaria, this breed is influenced by both Arabian and Thoroughbred stock. The Pleven variant is chestnut colored, with those horses ranging from dark chestnut to black referred to as Danubian. These animals are used both as saddle horses and as farm horses and average 15.2 hands in height.

POITEVIN (CHEVAL DU POITOU)

This breed was developed in France, and is used today primarily for breeding mules. As such, they are known informally as *molassier*, or mule-breeders. Poitevins are usually grey or dun-colored, and average 16.3 hands in height.

PONY OF THE AMERICAS

A spotted breed, the Pony of the Americas was established in 1956. The foundation sire, Black Hand, resulted from a cross between an Appaloosa mare and a Shetland stallion. In appearance, the Pony of the Americas has a conformation halfway between the Arabian and the Quarter Horse. The breed also has the distinctive coloring of the Appaloosa *(see Appaloosa).* A good jumper, the Pony of the Americas also makes an excellent trotting horse, and is often used in competitions for young riders. Its endurance and speed make it a good trekking mount for long distance riding and flat racing. This elegant horse stands 11.2 to 13 hands high. The breed is found in the United States and Canada, where there are 24 clubs and over 12,000 horses of the breed.

Below and at right: **Pony of the Americas foals. The Pony of the Americas was developed especially as a children's pony. It's a versatile and well-balanced pony. Colorations vary widely.** *Overleaf:* **A Pony of the Americas mare.**

POSTIER (See BRETON)

POTTOCK (BASQUE PONY)

The Pottock, whose name in Basque means literally 'small horse,' have been known for over a thousand years, but became a registered breed only in the 1970s. Typical of the small, sturdy mountain horses of southwestern Europe, the Pottock has no doubt been somewhat influenced by Arabian blood over the years. It stands 12 to 13 hands and ranges in color from brown to black, but occurs in other colors, such as bay or chestnut, though rarely in any but solid colors.

POZNAN

Native to Poland, this breed is used today primarily for racing. These horses are solid in color, and average 16 hands in height.

PREZEWALSKI'S HORSE

A native of the Dagin Shan (Yellow Horse) Mountain region of Mongolia's Gobi Desert, Prezewalski's Horse (*Equus prezewalskii*) is the only remaining *true wild horse* left on Earth. As such, it is a separate species of animal, completely distinct from all other living horses (*Equus caballus*).

The species takes its name from Colonel NM Prezewalski, who discovered it in 1881. Only about 50 remain in the wild, but at least 200 are in zoos. This sturdy animal measures about 12 hands in height and is dun-colored, with the lower part of the legs black and a black stripe down the center of its back. Other so-called wild horses are *feral*, ie, descendants of domesticated animals that have escaped.

PRUSSIAN (See TRAKHENER)

QUARTER HORSE

When the Quarter Horse is mentioned, one tends to think mainly of the American Wild West, but this breed can claim many sources, including origins in the eastern part of the United States. As with the development of so many other breeds, selective crossbreeding was used to develop this particular type. The goal was to produce a smaller, quicker, more compact type of horse, which would be dependable, and which would have a good disposition.

The Quarter Horse has a multitude of fields in which it excels — or at least holds its own — against other breeds. The most notable is racing. It excels in short races of 350 to 400 yards in distance, as well as in full quarter-mile races of 440 yards, and in doing so has garnered many of the largest purses in American racing! Probably the best known quarter-mile race is the All-American Futurity, which takes place at Ruidoso Downs in New Mexico. Until

Below and right: **Prezewalki's Horse, the only truly wild horse remaining on earth. All other 'wild horses' are more accurately termed 'feral,' or formerly domesticated breeds reverted to the wild. This horse is unique.**

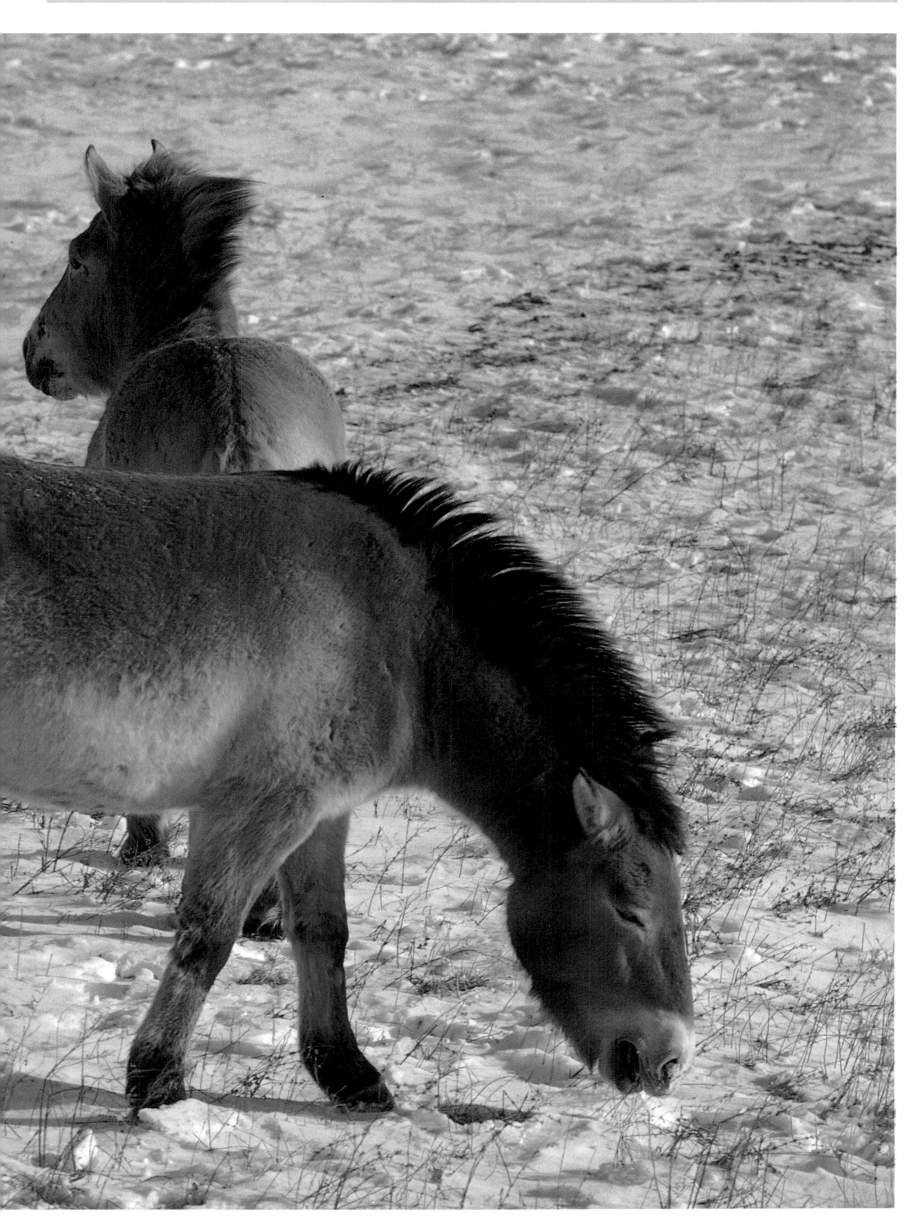

recently, when the Breeders Cup was inaugurated, it was the country's highest purse, even exceeding that of the Triple Crown races.

The 1988 running of this, the richest of all Quarter Horse races, took place at Ruidoso Downs on 5 September. The odds-on favorite at post time was *Sig Hanson*. However, he acted up considerably in the starting gate and this may have thrown his stride off somewhat. The winner was *Murganser*, whose share of the purse was an even *$1 million*. The filly *See Me Do It* was second and won $350,000. *Super DeKas* and *Sky Fire* finished in a dead heat for third—the show position—and won approximately $100,000 each. Every horse

continued on page 126

At right: Owner Bill Trapp and his Quarter Horse *King Ranch Quarter Commando,* an important stud in Australia's Northern Territory in the 1970s. *Below:* A Quarter Horse mare and two foals. *At far right and overleaf:* An American Quarter Horse. Note its buckskin coloration.

continued from page 122

in the race had to have made showings in top Quarter Horse races prior to this race in order to be qualified. *Every horse in the race won some money.* Three great stallions that have won this race in past years were *Dash To Cash*, *Easy Jet* and *Go Man Go*. In announcing the parents of the ten entrants before the race, the names of all three of these sires came up at least twice.

The first great Quarter Horse to gain a wide reputation was *Steel Dust*, foaled in Illinois in 1843 and taken to Lancaster, Texas three years later. Sired by *Harry Bluff* with his ancestry traced to *Sir Archy*, he was a blood bay, weighing about 1200 pounds. He earned such fame as a racehorse — and as a sire — that his descendants became noted as the best cow horses and running horses. In the following decades, the *Steel Dust* line of horses became well known all through the West. The name was quite common until the American Quarter Horse Association was founded in 1940, and the name 'Quarter Horse' was officially adopted.

Below: A Quarter Horse with coat sleek as a Saddlebred's. At bottom: A white Quarter Horse. At right: A bay chestnut Quarter Horse in a sportive pose.

Another very famous horse of the Quarter Horse line was *Peter McCue*, foaled in 1895, and owned and bred by Samuel Watkins of Petersburg, Illinois. He was first registered as a Thoroughbred, but it was later proven that his sire was *Dan Tucker*, who had been sired by *Shiloh*. *Peter McCue* stood for service in Texas, western Oklahoma and Colorado, and today most Quarter Horse lines trace to him. Of the 11,510 Quarter Horses registered before 1948, at least 2304 of them traced their male line to *Peter McCue*, through his sons, grandsons and great-grandsons. The only other horse that came close to *Peter McCue* in this regard was *Traveler*, who in 1948 could claim 749 descendants.

Many of the great Quarter Horse sires have their ancestry traced back to Thoroughbred mares or sires, rather than Quarter Horses. Examinations of the pedigrees reveal that very few of the earlier registrants did *not* carry some known Thoroughbred breeding close up in their pedigree. As a result, Quarter Horses vary greatly in size, because of they are bred for a specific type of use, rather than for specific characteristics. There is a very wide range in size, from 850 pounds to as much as 1300 pounds, depending upon the purpose for which they are bred.

continued on page 132

Below: A prosperous Montana rancher astride a Quarter Horse. *At right:* A San Francisco police officer and his Quarter Horse service mount. *At far right:* A Quarter Horse. *Overleaf:* A Quarter Horse with buckskin coloration.

continued from page 128

Quarter Horses are often described in two types: the 'Thorough-bred' type, and the 'Bull Dog' type. The former favors the Thoroughbred in appearance, although it is much more heavily muscled. The latter type has a more chunky conformation and is even more heavily muscled. In early Quarter Horse shows, great emphasis was placed on heaviness of muscling. Since about 1945, however, most winners have been in the middle range. Likewise, in quarter-mile racing, the Bull Dog type had been considered superior, but now opinion has swung to favor the Thoroughbred type. As great cutting horses, cow horses and those used in rodeos as dogging and roping horses, many of the Bull Dog type are favored because their great power enables them to quickly reach great speeds for short distances. Good cutting and roping horses generally stop with their hind feet, and can pivot either way, as they tend to keep their legs well under them.

For all rodeo events—from team roping to barrel racing—Quarter Horses are by far the most popular choice. For the working ranchman or for the youngster with his first mount, they meet the mark in Western riding. At the same time, they do an outstanding job for the outfitter or the dude rancher. Quarter Horse breeders and owners prefer dark or conservative colors in their animals. Off-color animals, such as pinto, appaloosa, or albino, are rejected by the American Quarter Horse Association. Formed in 1940 by a group of breeders in Fort Worth, Texas, today the Association's Quarter Horse Registry is the largest of any breed in the world, with more than 1.85 million horses listed.

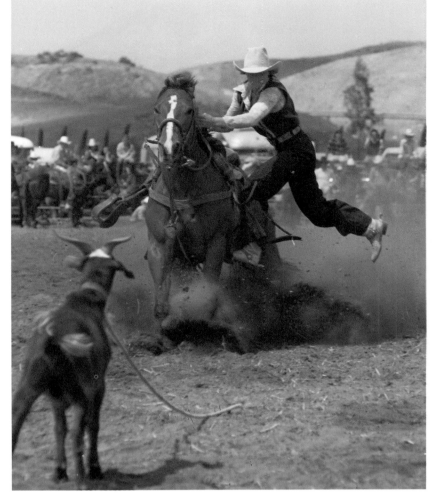

At right: **Goat roping with a Bull Dog-type Quarter Horse.** *Below:* **Calf roping with a Quarter Horse.** *At far right:* **A brown bay stallion.** *Below far right:* **A white Quarter Horse.** *Overleaf:* **Quarter Horses in dude ranch use.**

RHINELAND (RHINELAND HEAVY DRAFT, NIEDERSACHSEN HEAVY DRAFT)

This draft breed originated in the Rhine River valley of western Germany, with a stud book established in 1876. The Niedersachsen is generally considered identical, and the latter name is used only in Lower Saxony. Chestnut to roan in color, it averages 16 hands in height.

ROTTALER (See OLDENBURG)

RUSSIAN (SOVIET) HEAVY DRAFT

Despite its name, this breed is significantly smaller than the ubiquitous 16-hand class of European draft horses. This compact yet sturdy horse was developed under Tsar Nicholas II in the late nineteenth century, and is still common on Soviet collective farms today. Ranging in color from chestnut to roan, it averages only 14.2 hands in height, a hand smaller than the typical Thoroughbred or American Quarter Horse. The *Soviet* Heavy Draft, often referred to as a separate breed, averages 15.2 hands in height.

RUSSIAN TROTTER (See MÉTIS)

SABLE ISLAND PONY

These durable ponies take their name from a narrow, rugged island in the stormy North Atlantic Ocean, 200 miles southeast of the Canadian province of Nova Scotia. They originated from French horses left there in the eighteenth century, and number only about 300 today. They are solid in color and average 13 hands in height.

SADECKI (See WIELKOPOLSKI)

SALERNO (PERSANO)

This breed originated in 1763 in Naples, Italy during the reign of Charles III, and is used today primarily as a saddle horse. Solid in color, these large, powerful animals average 16 hands in height.

SANDALWOOD (See INDONESIAN)

SAN FRATELLANO (SAN FRATELLO)

The wild horse of Sicily's Nebrodi Mountains, the Sanfratellano proves to be an agreeable and hardy mount when domesticated. Ranging up to 16 hands, it is typically larger than most other semi-wild southern European mountain horses. This animal usually occurs in dark, solid colors, including black.

SANHO, SANPEITZE

(Subtypes of MONGOLIAN)

SARDINIAN

The rare, wild horse of Sardinia has been known historically since 1845, although the breed has probably been on this Mediterranean island since Roman times, or before. Like the other small mountain horses of southern Europe, such as the Bardigiano or the Garrano, this horse is well suited to difficult, rugged terrain. It ranges from bay to chestnut to black and stands up to 13 hands in height.

SCHLESWIG (SCHLESWIG HEAVY DRAFT)

This breed originated in the northern German state that is its namesake. Its stud book was established in 1871, but the breed has decreased in number since the turn of the century. Used today primarily for draft and farm work, this horse is usually chestnut in color, and averages 15.3 hands in height.

SCHWEIKEN (See KONIK)

At right, far right and overleaf: Three views of a 15-year old Shetland Pony mare named Blazer. Blazer is owned by Barbara Rebok of Lincoln, California.

SEINE INFÉRIEURE

This breed originated in northern France, and is used today as a saddle horse, as well as a draft horse. It ranges from bay or brown to roan, and averages 16 hands in height.

SELLE FRANÇAIS (NORMAN)

The Selle Français, or French Saddle Horse, boasts a wildly-mixed ancestry of Norman Draft Horse, German, Arabian and Barb blood, and it also can claim some two percent French Trotter, with a touch of Thoroughbred breeding. Although the breed was developed in the early nineteenth century, the stud book was not established until 1950. The Selle Français is used in several sports, including hunting, cross-country racing and flat racing. The Selle Français are typically bay or chestnut in color.

The breed is divided into two types—the medium weight and the heavy—which are further subdivided into a total of five groups. The medium-weight type includes small (up to 15.3 hands), medium (15.3 to 16.2 hands) and large (over 16.2 hands). The heavy type consists of the small group (up to 16.2 hands) and the large group (over 16.2 hands). The distinction between the medium-weight and the heavy types is based on the horse's ability to carry weight.

SENNER PONY

Now extinct, these small horses once inhabited the Teutoberg Forest near Hanover in Germany.

SHAGYA (See ARABIAN)

SHAN (See BURMESE)

SHETLAND PONY

Standing just nine to 10.2 hands, this little horse is one of the smallest breeds in the world. Few people fully realize, or appreciate, the value of this little animal, whose ancestors had such a hard life slaving in the mines and on the farms on the stormy Shetland Islands, located 250 miles north of northern Scotland and 350 miles south of the Arctic Circle. Because it was isolated since the Bronze Age from many horses except for rare contact with the Icelandic ponies, the Shetland is one of the purest breeds.

Much smaller than even the Welsh Pony, the Shetland is a very strong, rugged breed, which makes it ideal for use as a draft animal in coal mines and on farms. Seldom stabled in the very inclement climate of its native country, the Shetland's heavy coat nevertheless withstood these conditions quite well. When forage was scarce it would eat whatever was available, even seaweed.

The Shetland has long been bred for its pinto (or paint) coloring. Most commonly its coat contains white spots on a darker background. The Shetland's small size and gentle disposition has made it a long time favorite. As a riding animal or hitched to a cart, it can be used by people of all ages, even young toddlers. With its patient

continued on page 140

continued from page 136

disposition, the Shetland's value as a child's play partner is priceless. Furthermore, if a child falls from its back, there is little likelihood of an injury, as the distance to the ground is relatively small.

After they were brought south to Scotland, these agreeable characteristics became evident, and people began seriously breeding Shetlands. In 1890 the breeders formed the Shetland Pony Stud Book Society and produced Volume I of its stud book the following year. Two years earlier, in 1888, the American Shetland Pony Club had been formed, with Buffalo Bill Cody prominent among the 205 breeders listed in the United States. Robert Lilburn owned one of the largest herds in the United States, and registered more than 200 animals in 1906. A total of 425 pedigreed Shetlands were imported from Scotland the same year. Today, Canada, the Netherlands, Great Britain and parts of South America and Africa have Shetland Pony Clubs.

SHIRAZI (See DARASHOURI)

SHIRE

The Shire is a descendant of the Old English Heavy Horse, or Black Horse (aka Great Horse), often spoken of by horsemen as the largest breed of horses ever produced, standing 19 hands and weighing much more than a ton. Even today's Shires stand as tall as 17.3 hands and can weigh 1760 to 2650 pounds.

The modern Shire, though not quite up to carrying the knights of the Middle Ages, is the chief agricultural draft animal in both England and Canada. The Shires' most marked characteristics are large bones, short, strong backs and quarters that are heavy and powerful. Usually dark brown or black in color, the Shires' legs and pasterns are covered with long, thick hair. The horse's quick, graceful movements belie its enormous size, as does its disposition, which is quiet and unruffled. In pulling contests, the Shire rarely becomes excited and, like the Belgian and Clydesdale, can pull almost double its weight on a weighted skid!

In England the Shire Horse Society was formed in 1878. The American Shire Horse Breeders Association was formed in 1885. However, the Shire has not been as strongly favored in the United States, as it tends to be more sluggish than the other draft breeds and lacks their style. In addition, the excessive feathering on its legs and pasterns makes it compare less favorably to the Percheron and the Belgian. In addition to this latter feature, the Shire is characterized by dark (frequently dappled grey) color, with white markings.

SICILIAN

Having originated in the eastern part of Sicily from Arabian stock, the Sicilian is a durable riding or light draft horse that stands 15.1 to 15.3 hands in height. This compact horse ranges in color from bay to chestnut, and may also occur in black or dappled grey.

Below: **A Whitbread Ale dray, towed along by the brewery's dapple gray Shire Horses, in London.** *At right:* **A Shire Horse stallion with white stockings.**

SIGLAVY (See ARABIAN)

SKOGSRUSS (See GOTLAND)

SKYROS PONY

Averaging just over nine hands, the Skyros is probably the smallest nonmidget horse in the world. It was originally bred on the Greek island of Skyros, and is still used there as a pack animal, although its principal use outside the island is as a saddle animal for small children. It ranges in color from brown to grey.

SOKOLSK (SOKOLSKY)

This breed originated in Poland with Belgian Heavy Draft influence, and is used today only for farm work. These horses are usually chestnut in color, and average 15.3 hands in height.

SORRAIA

This semi-wild, ram-faced breed is found in the remote and mountainous regions of the northwestern Iberian peninsula. They are similar in appearance, and probably related, to the Tarpan of Eastern Europe. Sorraias are used today primarily for interbreeding with domestic horses. Inbred with Barbs in ancient times, they probably played a role in the development of the Arabian. These animals are generally dun-colored, and average 13 hands in height.

SOUTH GERMAN COLD BLOOD
(See NORIC)

SOVIET HEAVY DRAFT
(See RUSSIAN HEAVY DRAFT)

SPANISH MUSTANG (See MUSTANG)

SPANISH BARB (See BARB)

SPITI

Like the Tibetan horse to which it is closely related, the Spiti originated in the Himalayas. This pony is nearly always grey, with a fuller mane and tail than the Tibetan, and stands 12 hands in height.

STANDARDBRED

Descended from the great white English Thoroughbred stallion *Messenger* (1780), the Standardbred was developed in the nineteenth century specifically to become the American standard trotting horse. *Messenger* himself was descended from *Sampson* (1745), who had sired the founders of the French Trotting Horse lineage.

The Standardbred may range in color from bay to chestnut to black, with grey or roan Standardbreds being quite rare. Typically this horse stands 15.2 to 16 hands.

To qualify for registration as a Standardbred under the stud book, which was established in 1871, a horse must be the progeny of a registered Standardbred stallion and a registered Standardbred mare. The horse must pace a mile in less than 2:25 or trot a mile in 2:30. This is the 'standard' for the breed, thus the name. It should be noted that a pacer is slightly faster than a trotter, and very few horses can both pace and trot swiftly. However, the horse *Calumet Evelyn* by *Guy Albey* paced a mile in 1:59.4, and four days later trotted a mile in 2:00 flat, wearing the same shoes and without using toe plates or extra weights. The Standardbred is generally used for harness racing.

STRELETS ARAB (See ARABIAN)

At right: **A bay Standardbred stallion. Standardbreds are descended from the celebrated English Thoroughbred *Messenger*, and are bred for harness racing.**

SUFFOLK (SUFFOLK PUNCH)

Little has been recorded of the Suffolk's early history, except that it originated in 1506 and is probably related to the other draft breeds. The Suffolk is an exceptionally hard-working draft horse used mainly in Norfolk and Suffolk, though it is not nearly as well known nor as widely distributed as the Shire or Clydesdale.

Its body is long in proportion to its height, and its legs are more slender than those of the Shire and the Clydesdale, and free from long hair. The Suffolk is an easy-going horse, of mild disposition, and it usually leads a long life. Like the Shire, the Suffolk's coloring is normally bay or chestnut, and it usually stands 16.2 hands in height. In heavy pulling it proves a stubborn, determined breed, and will not give up the challenge easily. The Suffolk breed society was established in 1877.

SUMBA, SUMBAWA (See INDONESIAN)

SWEDISH WARM BLOOD

Sometimes called the Swedish Half Blood, this horse was developed during the seventeenth century with Arabian, Friesien and Thoroughbred blood. It is well known in international competition dressage, working hunter competition and combinations. This is a tall horse, usually more than 16.2 hands, and is most often found in dark, solid colors.

SYRIAN ARAB (See ARABIAN)

TARPAN

Thought to be the forerunner of all lightly built ('warm blooded') horses, the Tarpan once roamed from Poland to the Ukraine, where it was domesticated as a draft animal and occasionally hunted for meat. The last true Tarpan died in the Munich Zoo in 1887, eight years after this breed disappeared in the wild. Standing 13 hands, it ranged from dun colored to brown. A descendant of the Tarpan continues to survive in small numbers in captive breeding communities in Poland and elsewhere in eastern Europe.

TCHENARANI

This breed originated in Persia, and is used today primarily as a saddle horse. It may be found in any color, and averages 15 hands in height.

TENNESSEE WALKING HORSE

The Tennessee Walking Horse, like the Saddlebred, was developed in the southern United States more than a century ago as a horse to carry its rider at a very fast walking pace on property inspection tours. Primarily a product of Thoroughbred and Standardbred blood, its pace is very smooth and fluid, as well as swift — ranging from six to eight miles per hour — which makes it a perfect choice for the pleasure riding and showing it is used for today. As this animal glides along, it lifts its front feet, which usually are shod with shoes weighted in the front, very high. The official description of its gait is

At right: **A Tennessee Walking Horse with a forehead star.** *Below:* **Riders guide their Tennessee Walking Horses up a streambed on a pleasant day in Tennessee.**

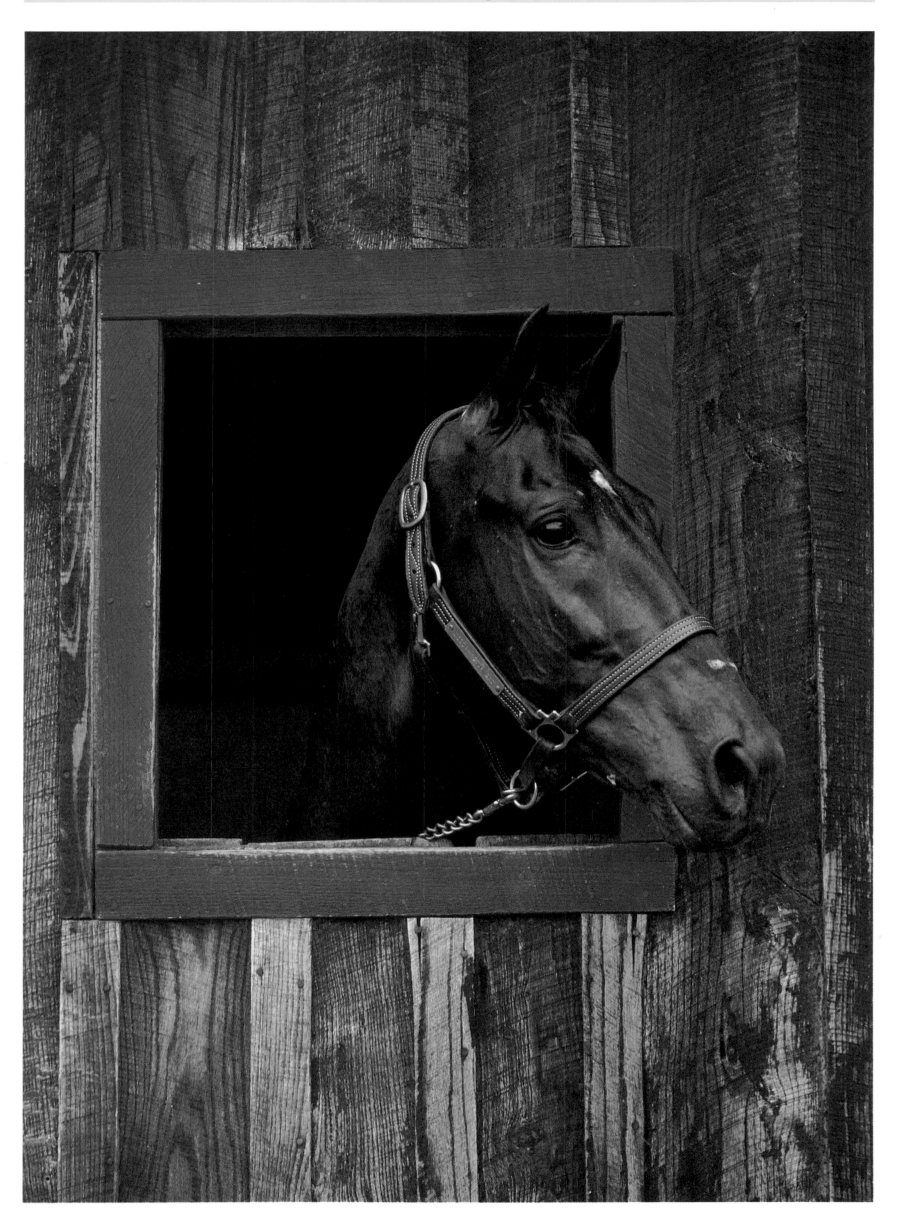

a 1 – 2 – 3 – 4 beat, with each of the four feet striking the ground at different times in regular intervals, such as: left front, right hind, right front, left hind.

The stallion *Black Allen*, which was foaled in 1886, is credited with starting this highly praised breed. *Black Allen*'s sire was the trotting stallion *Allendorf*, and his mother was a Morgan mare, *Maggie Marshall*. The Tennessee Walker was not recognized as a separate breed until 1910. The Tennessee Walking Horse Breeders Association was formed in 1935, with over 200,000 horses listed by 1984.

One horse that has greatly influenced the improvement of the breed is *Roan Allen-38*; it is common for the greatest horses developed in this breed to trace their ancestry to *Roan Allen-38*, who was descended from *Allen F-1*, a Standardbred.

At right: A Tennessee Walking Horse in competition. *Below: Pride's Generator*, a sire owned by Claude Crowley of Salem, Missouri. *At far right:* The Tennessee Walking Horse *Coin's Hard Cash*, which was the 1987 World Grand Champion.

One reason for the rapid rate of improvement of the breed is that they are in constant show ring exposure with strong competition. In horse shows, they are expected to perform three distinct gaits: the walk, the running walk and the canter. The walk must be a good, flat-footed walk at a rate of four to five miles an hour. The running walk is the gait that sets this breed apart from all other breeds. It starts as a flat-footed walk with a diagonally opposed foot movement and, as the speed increases to seven or eight miles per hour, the hind foot begins stepping eighteen inches ahead of the spot that the front foot on that side had just left. This stride gives a gliding sensation to the rider. The third gait, the canter, is an easy gallop with a rocking, or rolling motion. Most people refer to it as a 'rocking chair gait,' because it is so smooth and comfortable for the rider.

In show competition, the front shoes of the Tennessee Walker are built up and weighted to induce the horse to pick the front feet up higher as it moves. The watchwords in training are 'correct stride and action!'

Tennessee Walking Horses. *At right and below:* **With riders at a competition.** *Below right:* **A white-faced Walking Horse.** *Overleaf:* **In a presentation stance.**

TERSK (TEREK, TERSKY)

The horse of the Cossacks, this stunningly handsome silver-grey breed originated in the Caucasus region of the Soviet Union. In the nineteenth century, they were further developed by Count Strovanov, and in the 1920s, they were bred by Marshal Budyonny, who also developed the breed that bears his name. This breed is used today primarily as a saddle horse, and is distinguished by its color rather than size, which varies widely.

THOROUGHBRED

The development of the Thoroughbred as a racehorse began in England. Although the Romans and the Normans had brought horses with them on their conquests, the English, despite their vast economic resources, lacked competent direction, and so went about improving the quality of their horses in a rather haphazard manner. During the reign of Elizabeth I (1558–1603), armor was used less and less, but the Heavy Horse, which had carried outfitted knights into battle, still remained in demand. Realizing the problem, Queen Elizabeth, at the suggestion of the Duke of Leicester, called to her court Don Prospero d'Osma of Naples, who at the time was reputed to be the leading specialist in the field of horse breeding. (The Italians were well known for creating fine breeds of horses by selective breeding.) From the very beginning, the goal was to create a breed with both speed and endurance. In 1576 d'Osma wrote a report on the English stud, making special mention of two mares with Italian names, *Brilladoro* and *Savoia*, as likely to produce fast running foals if bred to good stallions.

Below: **A chestnut Thoroughbred colt with two white stockings.** *At right:* **A beautiful Thoroughbred stallion with a blaze face and one white stocking.**

Three stallions are credited as the foundation sires of the Thoroughbred: *Godolphin Barb*, *Byerly Turk* and *Darley Arabian*. *Godolphin Barb* was foaled about 1724 on the Barbary Coast of North Africa and brought to France, then later to England. It is probable that *Byerly Turk* came to England in about 1689. *Darley Arabian* came to England from Arabia via Spain in 1706.

The most famous and best known of the founding stallion line was *Eclipse*, a grandson of *Darley Arabian*. Thus, it can be seen that the Arabian horse had an important part in founding the Thoroughbred line, just as it had in other breeds. In turn, the Thoroughbred influenced the founding of other breeds, such as the Standardbred and the Quarter Horse. The first stud book was published in 1791 by J Weatherby as the Weatherby Stud book, entitled 'An Introduction to a General Stud Book.' The General Stud Book has been kept up to date since then. Many great Thoroughbred horses developed in the United States and some other countries cannot be traced for entry into the General Stud Book. Three of these were *Commando*, *Lexington* and *Hanover*. However, such horses could be raced in England only as 'half bred' horses.

At right: **A trainer and and a groom wash down a bay-colored Thoroughbred.** *Below:* **Training a Thoroughbred.** *Opposite:* **A spirited Thoroughbred foal.**

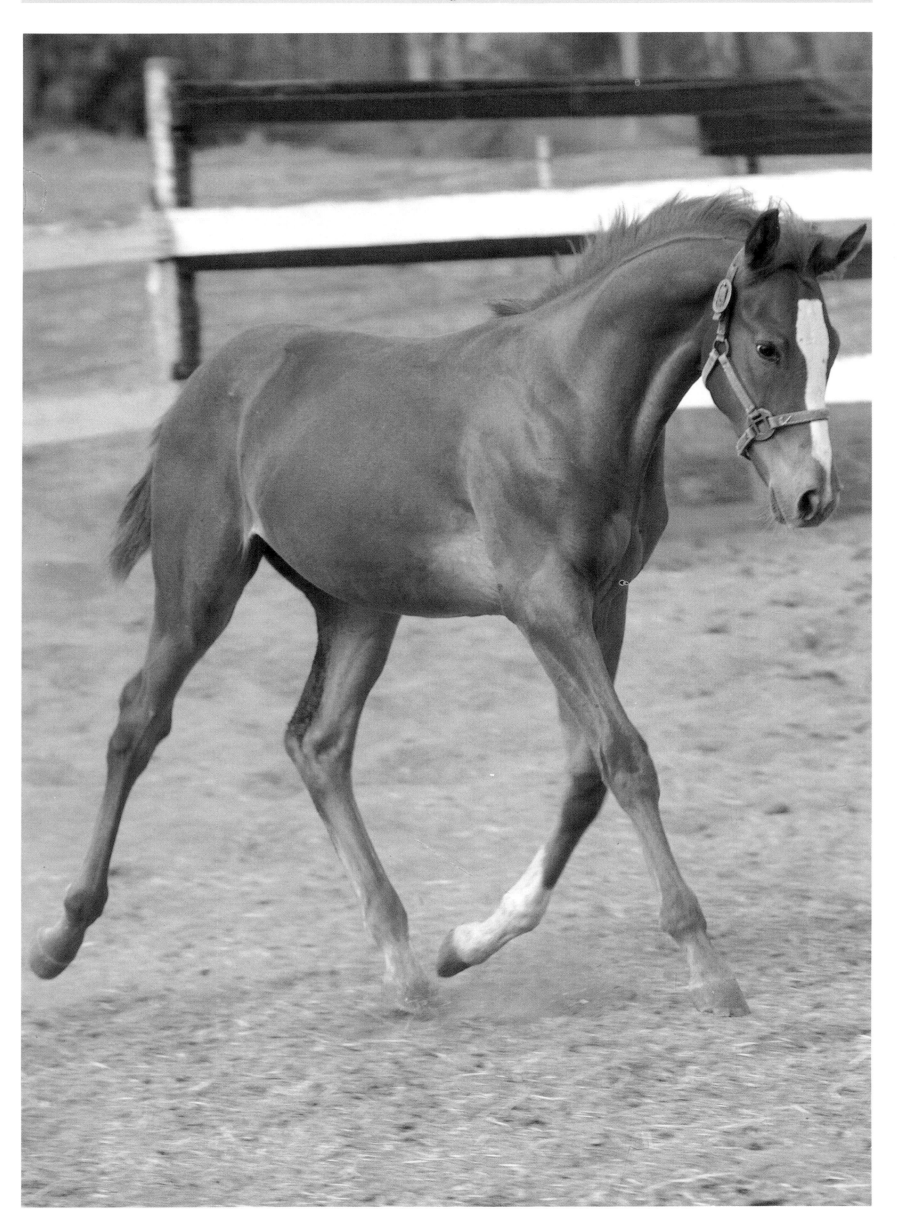

Much has been written about *Eclipse* and his outstanding track records. He came from the best of lines, sired by *Marske*. His mother, *Spiletta*, was sired by the *Godolphin Barb*. Eclipse was a liver chestnut with a long white blaze on his face and a long white stocking on one hind leg. Although considered poorly built by horsemen because he had a very long neck and was built low in the front, his legs and quarters were good and his chest was well formed. From an early age he showed signs both of great speed and great unmanageability. His owner, finally despairing of his unruly temperament, put him up for auction, whereupon he was purchased by a meat salesman named Wildman for 75 guineas. Wildman tried many methods of breaking the colt of his difficult ways and, failing, made a deal with a Captain O'Kelley, a sportsman, who employed a very good trainer by the name of Sullivan. Sullivan was known as 'the charmer' because of his seemingly magical way with troublesome horses. As compensation for arranging to have Sullivan train him, O'Kelley was to receive a half interest in *Eclipse*. Sullivan's methods *did* live up to their reputation, and under his management *Eclipse* became a docile horse.

Eclipse was not raced until he was five years old. On 3 May 1769 he was entered in a four-mile race (6400 meters). He ran the distance in six minutes, easily winning over a field of strong competitors. O'Kelley now was sole owner of *Eclipse*, having purchased Wildman's half share. In *Eclipse*'s second race, O'Kelley bet all the other owners 1000 guineas each that his horse would win the four-mile race by at least one-eighth mile. He gave them two-to-one odds. *Eclipse* won handily by more than an eighth of a mile and O'Kelley collected his bets. *Eclipse* continued to race for two more years, between May 1769 and October 1770. He won all 26 of his races, setting numerous records. Then he was retired to stud, with a fee of 1000 pounds. Many of today's great racehorse bloodlines proudly trace their ancestry to *Eclipse*.

Below: **A Thoroughbred at a gallop at Two Creek Ranch in Texas.** *At right:* **A closeup of horse and rider.**

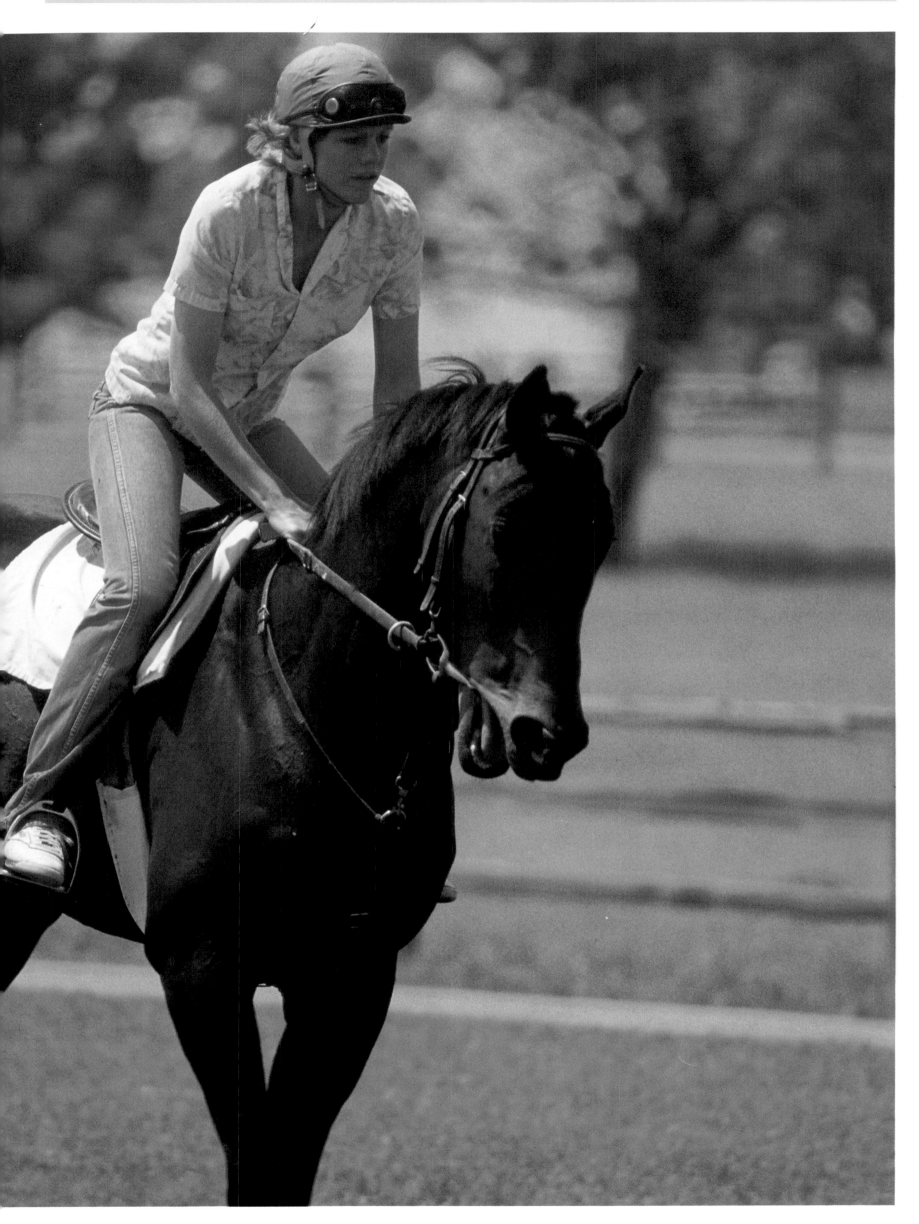

Secretariat

Secretariat was sired by *Bold Ruler* and foaled by *Something Royal* just after midnight on 10 March 1970, at the Meadow Stud Farm in Doswell, Virginia, just south of Richmond. Howard Gentry, manager of the farm, and a friend were playing pool nearby so they could be on hand to keep watch and give the mare any needed assistance with the birth. As it turned out, their assistance was indeed needed, as her fourteenth foal was a very large one. The foal was a chestnut with three white feet — and was able to stand at the age of one hour and 15 minutes.

Penny Tweedy, the owner of Meadow Farm in Caroline County, did not have high regard for *Secretariat* during his first two years. Her pride and joy was her great horse *Riva Ridge*. *Secretariat* did well in his early races, although he was beaten by several colts of his age.

On 5 May 1973, in the 99th Kentucky Derby, *Secretariat* would fully manifest his true colors. Trained by Lucian Lourin and ridden by Ron Turcotte, he ran a moderate first quarter mile in 25.2, compared to the 23.4 posted by *Sherry Greene*, the leader at that point. In the second quarter mile both were timed at 24 flat, but *Secretariat* was still practically last. In the third quarter mile, his time was 23.8, as he passed *Forego* and *Twice a Prince*. His time in the fourth quarter mile was 23.6, and by this time, he had disposed of *Navajo*, *Warbucks* and *Restless Jet*. Through the next eighth mile he passed *Angle Light*, a horse that had run a quarter in the Wood Memorial in 22 flat, besting *Secretariat* in that race. In this eighth-mile he also passed *Our Native*, *Gold Bug*, *Shecky Greene*, and *Royal Regal*, leaving only one-eighth, and *Sham*! In the final eighth mile, he and *Sham* ran side by side as a team for 100 yards. Then, in the last 120 yards, the remainder of the final eighth, *Secretariat* made his rush and beat *Sham* by two and one-half lengths! He had run the final quarter in 23 flat, making his time 1:59.4. (The all-time record for the Kentucky Derby had been two minutes flat, set by *Northern Dancer* in 1964.)

In the second leg of the Triple Crown, the Preakness, *Secretariat* again bested *Sham* by two and one-half lengths. *Our Native* was third, the same order in which the three had finished in the Kentucky Derby. *Secretariat*'s finish was so swift and so spectacular that the spectators were shocked when the tote board showed his time as 1:55 — a full second slower than the track record of 1:54 set by *Cananero II*. Suspicion of the electric board was aroused, and the clocker from the paper, *The Daily Racing Form*, Gene (Frenchy) Schwartz and the paper's chief clocker at Pimlico Racetrack, Frank Robinson, both claimed that they had clocked the race in 1:55.4. The television network which had broadcast the race became involved and compared their videotapes of this race to those of the *Cananero II* Preakness run. This hypothetical race showed *Secretariat* beating *Cananero II* by about two lengths. The network claimed proof of a new track record.

Secretariat's most exciting and spectacular finish, however, was in the Belmont Stakes, the last of the Triple Crown races. His time in the race by eighths is as follows: 12.2; 11.4; 11.4; 11.2; 12 flat; 11.6; 12.2; 12.2; 12 flat; 12.8; 12.2; 12.8. His final eighth mile was done in 12.8, after he had eased up. Despite this, his speed on the earlier parts of the race gave him a clocking of two minutes, 11.2 seconds for the first mile and five-eighths, in which he beat *Swaps'* world record for one and five-eighths mile by two seconds. He had run the Derby distance of a mile and a quarter in one minute, 59 seconds, two-tenths seconds faster than his own earlier Derby record. He had run the mile and one-half Belmont in two minutes, 24 seconds, and finished *31 lengths* ahead of *Twice A Prince*, who was second, and 45 lengths ahead of *Sham*, who was last. At the end of the first mile of the race, *Sham* was running second, 20 lengths ahead of the rest of the field. Afterward it was discovered the gallant *Sham* had suffered a hairline fracture of the cannon bone. He was retired to stud. The previous record for the Belmont was two minutes, 26 and three-fifths seconds, set by *Gallant Man* in 1957.

Fifteen years after his amazing 1973 season, *Secretariat* was still well and working as a stud on the Gainesway Farm in Kentucky.

At right: The great Thoroughbred, **Secretariat**.

John Henry

Before point system payments were initiated for Triple Crown winners and horses that place and show, and before the present day Breeders Cup awards, *John Henry*, foaled in 1975, stood alone as the top Thoroughbred money winner.

The story is told of a couple who raised vegetables for a living in northern Kentucky, horse enthusiasts desirous of buying a stallion to stand at stud. One day they attended a horse auction in Lexington and discovered one stallion on the list that was very unpopular because of his disposition: he turned murderous around any other male horse who had the misfortune to cross his path. Needless to say, he was shunned by potential buyers. This couple bid $900 for him, all the money they had with them.

At the same auction was a two year old colt named *John Henry*, who sold for $25,000. At the end of the day the couple learned who their newly acquired stallion really was: the sire of the colt *John Henry*! As all horse lovers know, *John Henry* became almost unbeatable on turf, and fully unbeatable as a money winner. He won the Arlington Million at the age of nine, with his share of the million being $600,000. By the time he was retired in 1984, he had won 39 of 83 races, and his winnings had reached $6,597,947.

As the story goes, when *John Henry* began to amass his fortune, the couple who had fortunately purchased his sire were able to raise his stud fees — and stop raising vegetables!

Man o' War

Man o' War was one of the greatest racehorses of all time. Although he was never entered in the Kentucky Derby, he won both the Belmont Stakes and the Preakness in 1920, winning the former by 20 lengths! In 21 races as a two-year-old and as a three-year-old in the 1919 and 1920 seasons, he placed second only once — and then by only half a length.

Sired in 1917 by *Fair Play* at the Glen Riddle Farm, his breeder was August Belmot. The fiery chestnut stallion retired to the Hinata Stock Farm near Lexington in 1920, and moved in 1922 to nearby Faraway Farm, where he lived until his death in November 1947. Though his career was short and he never had a chance to run for the roses at Churchill Downs, *Man o' War* had a record which is considered truly legendary.

Below right: **The legendary *Man o' War* as a three-year-old in 1920. Clarence Kummer, in the saddle, rode this famous Thoroughbred in nine of his 11 races that season.** *Below left:* **A Thoroughbred colt shows an alert eye.** *Below, at bottom:* **Thoroughbred foals.** *At right:* **Thoroughbreds and their keeper.**

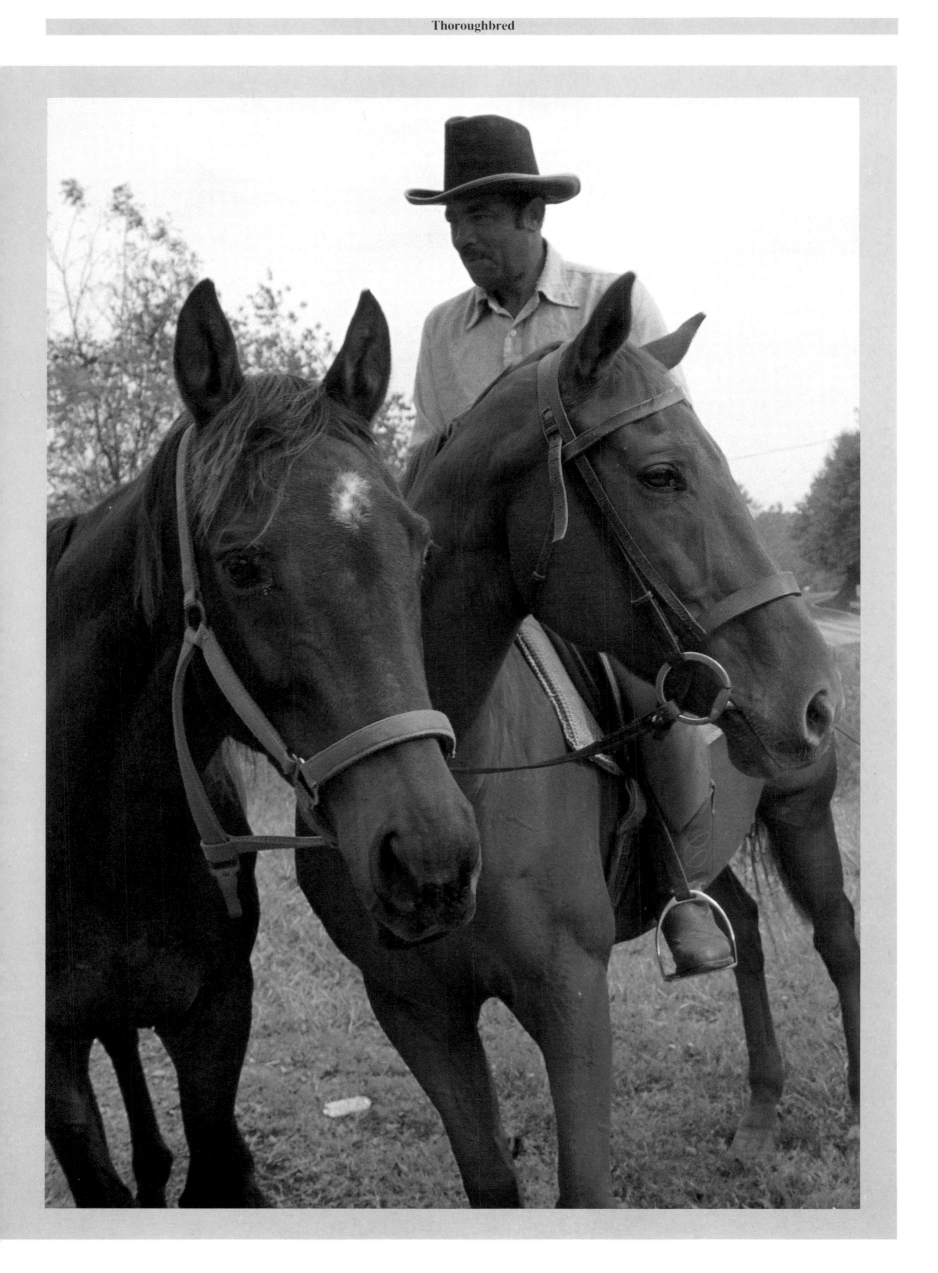

TIBETAN

This small breed originated high in the Himalayas, probably from Mongolian and Chinese stock, and is used today by the people of the region primarily as a pack and saddle horse. Generally dun-colored, this pony averages 12.2 hands in height.

TIMOR (See INDONESIAN)

TOBIANO (See PINTO)

TORIC

This breed originated in the small eastern European nation of Estonia, on the shores of the Baltic Sea, and is used today primarily as a harness and draft animal. This horse is bay or chestnut with white markings, and averages 15.1 hands in height.

TRAIT

The term 'Trait' is used as a prefix on most French draft breeds. These animals are listed herein by their specific breed names.

TRAIT DU NORD

As implied by the name, which literally means 'draft horse of the North,' this especially hardy breed originated in northeastern France, and is used today primarily as a draft animal. There was a great deal of Belgian and Ardennes influence prior to establishment of the stud book in 1919. This dark colored horse is approximately 16 hands in height.

TRAKEHNER

The Trakehner, formerly known as the East Prussian, is known for its smooth temperament, refined looks and graceful movement. The name of the breed is taken from the name of the *Trakehnen* Stud Farm, established in 1732 by Friedrich Wilhelm I of Prussia, when he added top quality Arabians to his breeding stock. His son, Frederick the Great, also took an avid interest in the horses, but after his death in 1786 the breeding operation was taken over by the state. Subsequently, the breeding policy was modified to produce only cavalry horses.

Below: **An illustration of a trooper of the Prussian Leib Dragoon Regiment, circa 1740. The trooper's horse is a Trakehner.** *At right:* **A contemporary Trakehner, with refined features. They are extremely good saddle horses.**

The breed survived the various wars of the area, however, and by the late 1930s there were some 25,000 mares belonging to 15,000 breeders. In 1945, at the end of the Second World War, as the Russians occupied what was formerly the German state of East Prussia, many owners gathered their belongings, including their horses, and fled to what is now West Germany. However, only 1500 Trakehners reached the West. By this time the breed had been lightened and improved by crossing with high quality Polish Arabian stock, to produce the dignified Trakehner we know today. Trakehners are 16 to 16.2 hands in height and range in color from chestnut to bay to black.

TURKOMAN (TURKMENE)

This breed originated in the Turkestan region of the Soviet Union, and is closely related to the Akhal-Teké and the Iomud. It is used today primarily as a saddle and race horse. This elegant horse ranges in color from black, grey or silver, to brown or gold. It averages 15.1 hands in height.

VIATKA

Subdivided into the Kasanski and Obvinski types, these horses were originally bred in Estonia, Latvia and Lithuania. All-purpose animals still used in farming, Viatkas average 13.2 hands in height. They are usually dark colored and often have a dark dorsal stripe and zebra markings.

VLADIMIR HEAVY DRAFT

Developed in the late nineteenth century concurrently with the Russian Heavy Draft, the Vladimir was also influenced by the Percheron, as well as Suffolk, Clydesdale and Shire stock. However, the breed was not standardized until 1946. This breed is somewhat larger than the Russian Heavy Draft, standing 15 to 16 hands, and is generally dark colored — ranging to black — with white markings, particularly on its well-feathered pasterns.

VORONESCH

This breed originated in the Soviet Union, and is used today as a saddle or draft horse. These horses range from bay or chestnut, to black in color, and average 15.3 hands in height.

WALER

Named for the state of New South Wales, this breed was originally developed in Australia in the late eighteenth century. The first horses to reach Australia arrived in 1788, but there are no exact records of what breeds were represented. However, after that date regular shipments of horses arrived from England, mostly believed to be a mixture of Arabians and Barbs, as well as Basuto ponies. These horses were used for expeditions into deserts and mountains, as well as for pulling coaches and carts, and clearing and plowing land.

Below: **A contemporary Waler, showing Thoroughbred influence, yet still an Australian type.** *Above right:* **The Waler as a stock horse: Bryan Wormwell on** *Joken.* **Below right:** **Richard Folp riding the Waler** *Yarramine Swagman.*

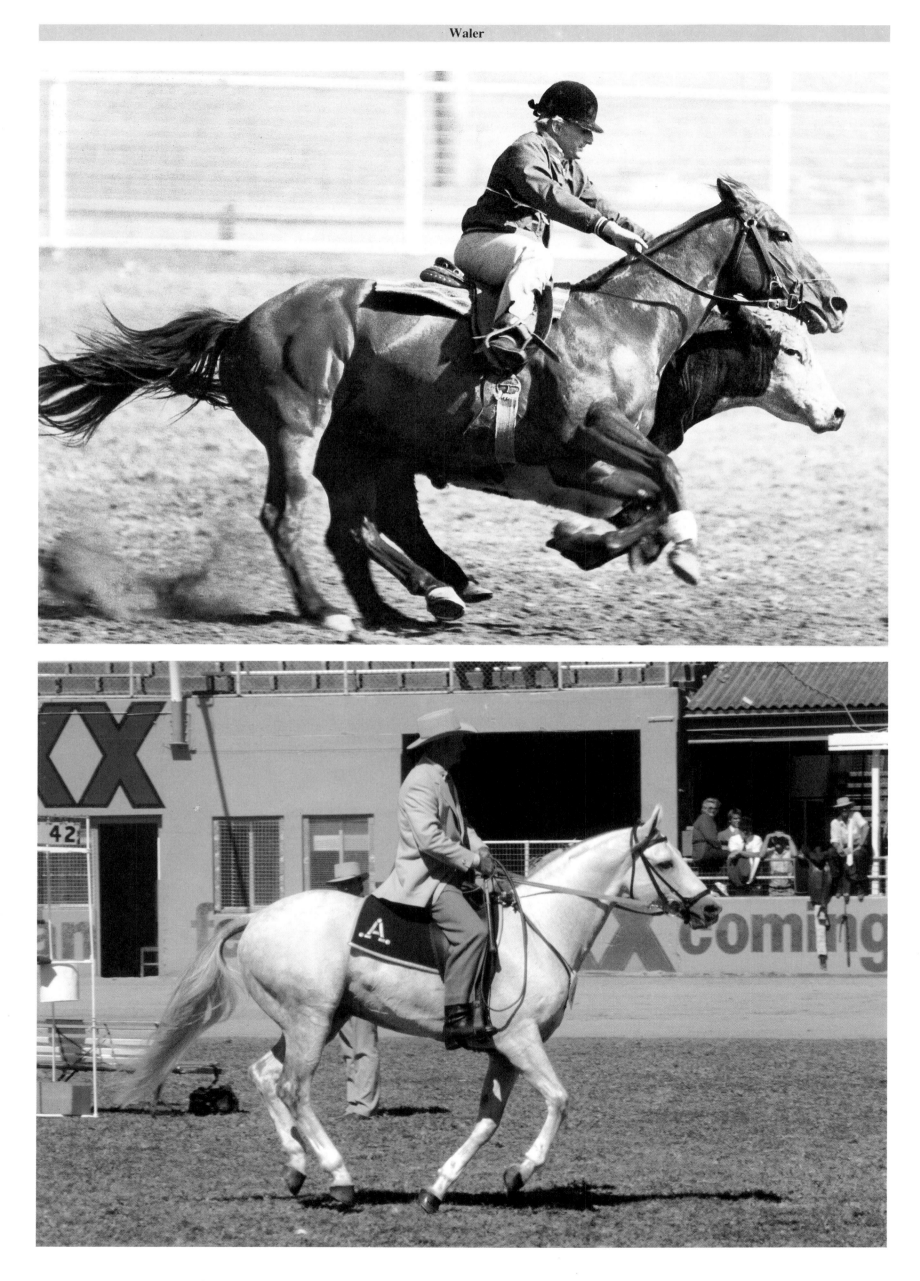

Racing also began to gain popularity, with the first official meeting being held in October 1810 in Sydney, and soon Thoroughbreds and Arabians were being imported from England to breed better racehorses. This led to an improvement in the bloodlines of working horses as well, and soon Australia began to breed stock and working horses of a distinctive type. These horses, which were soon known as the Australian Walers, are hardy, light in frame, have plenty of stamina and a willing temperament.

They stand between 15 and 16 hands, with good bone conformation. They are capable of carrying heavy weight all day and yet are nimble, with a turn of speed. Until World War I, when 121,344 horses were taken to the battlefields and used as cavalry mounts, they were used mainly for stock work. Sadly, the end of the war saw the near extinction of these fine horses, and in 1971 an organization was belatedly established to perpetuate the breed from the few remaining examples.

WELSH PONY
(COB TYPE, WELSH PONY and WELSH MOUNTAIN PONY)

These three types are basically identical except for size, and are classified into sections *by* size in the Stud Book of the Welsh Pony and Cob Society, which was first issued in 1900. The Welsh Mountain Pony (Section A) stands no taller than 12 hands. Both the Welsh Pony (Section B) and Welsh Pony of Cob Type (Section C) may range up to 13.2 hands, but the latter are heavier and sturdier than those in Section B.

Section D is the Welsh Cob, a larger version of the Welsh Pony of Cob Type. This horse stands 14.2 to 15.2 hands. Since 1946, when the Welsh Pony Society of America was formed, only Sections A and B have been valid in the United States.

Below: A high-spirited Welsh Pony shows its good lines, which betray some Arabian influence. *At right:* A closeup of a Welsh Pony with a facial stripe.

These animals are solidly colored, usually a dark hue. and are known to be well-built, intelligent animals. Although there is strong evidence to support the theory that their ancestry goes back to medieval times, after World War II there were only three stallions in existence. Since that time, however, their numbers have blossomed and they have been exported to countries all over the world, including places as far away as Australia.

During the eighteenth and nineteenth centuries, the Welsh Mountain Horse had become so inbred that Thoroughbred, Arabian and Hackney stallions were employed to build up the strain, but the most improvement in this breed seems to come from the Arabian. Thus today, the Welsh Mountain Pony tends to favor Arabian characteristics in its head, its tail carriage, its spirit and gait.

WESTLANDS PONY (See FJORD PONY)

WESTPHALIAN (See HANOVERIAN)

WIELKOPOLSKI (MALAPOLSKI)

These two breeds have been developed in Poland (in the respective regions of the same names) as riding horses, and the Malapolski is also a particularly good jumper. Each breed manifests the strong influence of both Oriental and Thoroughbred blood. In the Malapolski, there are two types according to size: the Sadecki (16.2 hands) and the Darbowsko-Tarnowski (15.3 hands).

WORONESCH (See VORONESCH)

WUCHUMUTSIN (See MONGOLIAN)

WÜRTTEMBERG

The Württemberg is a medium-sized horse, standing 15 to 16 hands high and weighing from 1000 to 1200 pounds. Although its stud book registration goes back only to 1895, this breed originally developed in Württemberg nearly 400 years ago from Arabian and Suffolk stock.

Since World War II its quality has been magnificently increased by further crossbreeding with Thoroughbreds and Arabians, making it much sought after as a sport and show horse. Similar to the Prussian Trakehner, the Württemberg boasts an excellent appearance, as well as grace in action.

YEMEN ARABIAN (See ARABIAN)

ZEMAITUKA (PECHORA)

Descending from the primitive wild horses of the Asiatic steppes, the Zemaituka of Lithuania is a sturdy animal with the ability to withstand cold temperatures. As a pack animal, it can typically travel 40 miles in one day. It stands up to 13.2 hands, and while it can be any color, its primitive heritage is evident in its black dorsal stripe.

Below: **A Welsh Mountain Pony with Arabian dapple coloring and a white face.**
At right: **A piebald Welsh Pony. Note its alert eyes and refined stance.**

APPENDICES

HORSE RACING

One of the most popular sports in the world is the one known simply as 'The Sport of Kings.' Horse racing as an avocation was almost certainly born within a matter of days, if not hours, after the first domestication of the horse many thousands of years ago. History shows that it existed as an organized event in Egypt and the Middle East, and Homer even describes a horse race in *The Iliad* (xxiii). By the late Middle Ages Newmarket in England was hosting regular, organized races. Horse racing is known to date from 1540 on the Roodee at Chester in England.

The first king known to enjoy 'The Sport of Kings' on a regular basis was James I of England (1566-1625), who attended races at Newmarket as early as 1605.

During the reign of George II (1727–1760), organized racing made its first appearance in America. Organized racing developed first in Virginia and the Carolinas, and has remained important in these areas ever since. George Washington, one of Virginia's pre-eminent citizens, was also a well-known horse breeder. Kentucky had become an important breeding center by 1795, and in the north, important races were first held on Long Island in 1819.

The early races were generally in the *four* mile class, but by 1880, those of distances less than *two* miles became the rule. By the turn of the century — in part because of the grueling four-mile races — racing was made illegal in all American states except Maryland and Kentucky. After 1920, however, 'The Sport of Kings' enjoyed a revival and was legalized once again.

Today the two most important annual events in the world of horseracing are the American and British Triple Crowns. The American Triple Crown consists of three individual races, which are, themselves, three of the most important single races in America. These are the Kentucky Derby (first run in 1875), the Preakness Stakes (first run in 1876) and the Belmont Stakes (first run in 1869). They are open to three-year-old colts, geldings or fillies and are a mile and a quarter, a mile and three-sixteenths, and a mile and a half in length, respectively.

Since it was first accomplished in 1919, only eleven horses have won all three races of the American Triple Crown. They are *Sir Barton* (1919), *Gallant Fox* (1930), *Omaha* (1935), *War Admiral* (1937), *Whirlaway* (1941), *Count Fleet* (1943), *Assault* (1946), *Citation* (1948), *Secretariat* (1973), *Seattle Slew* (1977), and *Affirmed* (1978).

The British Triple Crown consists of the straight mile at Newmarket, run during the first week of May, the 2641-yard Derby at Epsom, run on the first Wednesday in June, and the mile and three-quarters, run at Doncaster in September. The entire British Triple Crown was first won by *West Australian* in 1853, and his feat has been equaled by only 14 colts since then. These are: *Gladiateur* (1865), *Lord Jim* (1866), *Ormonde* (1886), *Common* (1891), *Isinglass* (1893) *Galtee More* (1897), *Flying Fox* (1899), *Diamond Jubilee* (1900), *Rock Sand* (1903), *Pommern* (1915), *Gay Crusader* (1917), *Gainsborough* (1918) and *Bahram* (1935).

Other important triple crowns include those in Ireland, Canada, Argentina, Japan and West Germany. The Irish Triple Crown consists of the Irish 200 Guineas (1921), the Irish Derby (1866) and the Irish St Leger (1915), which are a mile, a mile and a half and a mile and three-quarters, respectively.

The Canadian Triple Crown consists of the Queens Plate, the Prince of Wales Stakes and the Breeders' Stakes. The former is a mile and a quarter, and the latter two are a mile and a half.

The Argentine Triple Crown consists of the Polla de Potrillos, the Gran Premio Jocky Club, and the Gran Premio Nacional, which are 1600, 2000 and 2500 meters, respectively.

The Japanese Triple Crown includes the Satsuki Shou, Tokyo Yuushun (Tokyo Derby) and the Kikuka Shou, which are 2000, 2400 and 3000 meters, respectively.

The German Triple Crown races are the oldest in continental Europe, having been first run between 1869 and 1881. These

Previous pages: Cowboy and Quarter Horse. *Below:* Thoroughbreds close in on the finish line of Louisville, Kentucky's Churchill Downs, where the Kentucky Derby is run. *At right:* A Thoroughbred and its jockey at Churchill Downs.

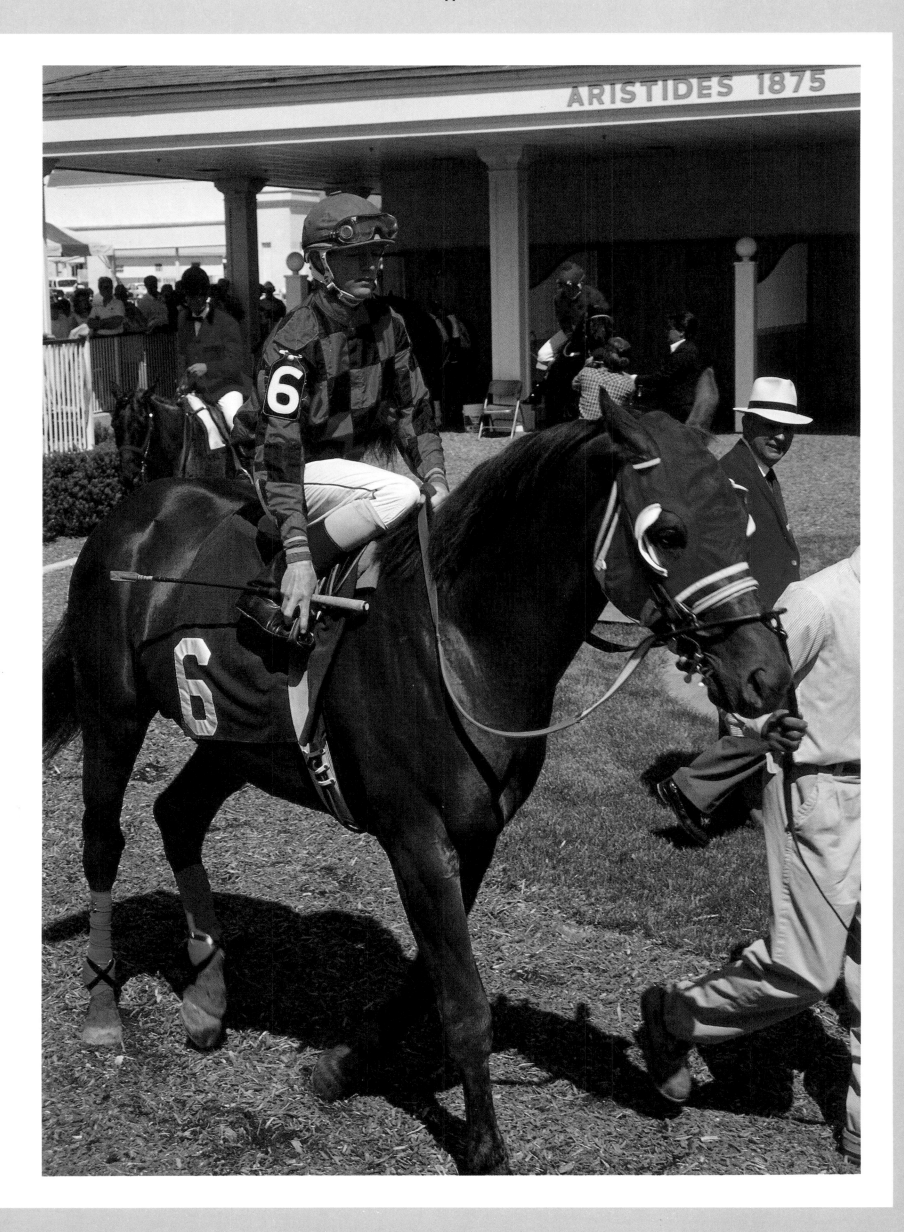

races are the Henckel-Rennen at Gelsenkirchen (1600 meters), the Deutsches Derby at Hamburg (2400 meters) and the Deutsches St Leger at Dortmund (2800 meters).

Elsewhere in Europe, specifically in France and Italy, there are tripartite racing events that are de facto 'triple crowns' which are not specifically known or run as such, although they are the equivalent of such triads in Germany and Britain. In France, the three races are the Poule d'Essai, the Prix du Jockey-Club, and the Prix Royal-Oak. In Italy, there are the Premio Parioli, the Derby Italiano and the St Leger Italiano.

In Australia, the premier races are the 2050 meter WS Cox Plate, run at Moonee Valley near Melbourne, and the 3200 meter Melbourne Cup, held at Flemington.

Run in May at Churchill Downs in Louisville, Kentucky, the Kentucky Derby, with its multimillion dollar purse, is the most important race in America, and perhaps the world. The fastest time for the mile and a quarter race was 1:59.4, run by *Secretariat*, who went on to win the entire Triple Crown in 1973. In so doing, *Secretariat* beat the time of *Northern Dancer*, who had set a record of two minutes flat in 1964. No horse has come close to *Secretariat*'s time since.

In England there is no horse race more important than the Derby, the race from which the Kentucky race takes its name. The Derby itself takes its name from the Earl of Derby, who first sponsored the race in 1780. Like the newer race at Churchill Downs, the Derby is open to three-year-olds. The course was intended to be one mile and a half (2640 yards), but instead is 2641 yards due to a survey error. Except for six years during World War II, when the race was held at Newmarket, the Derby has been held annually on the first Wednesday of June at Epsom Downs near London.

Other important English races are the two mile and a quarter Ascot Gold Cup, inaugurated in 1807, the two and a half mile Goodwood Cup, organized in 1812, and the two mile, five furlong Doncaster Cup, which dates from 1766, making it perhaps the oldest major race in the world.

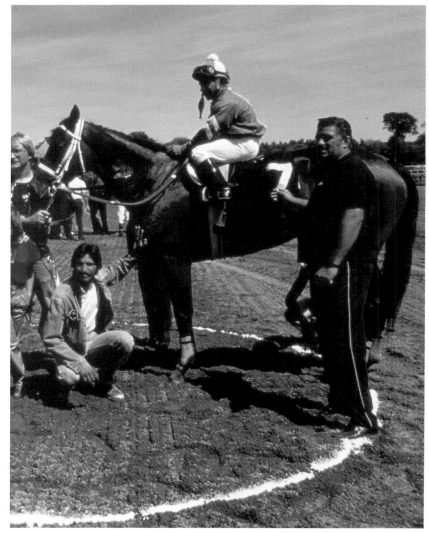

Above: **Admirers surround a racehorse at Saratoga, New York — home to the Travers, America's oldest racing event.** *Below:* **Ireland's Curragh racetrack.**

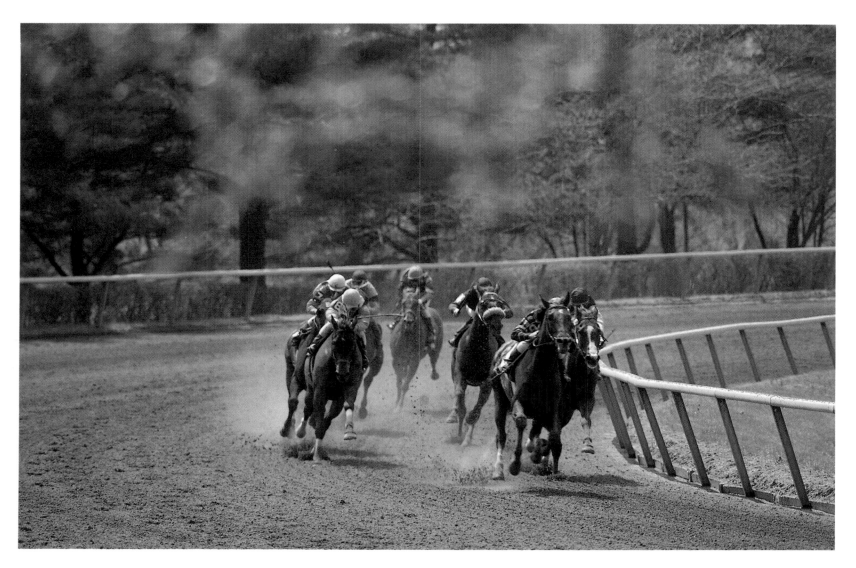

Below: An event on the grass at Saratoga. *Above:* A Thoroughbred race at Lexington, Kentucky — in 'bluegrass country,' known for fine Thoroughbreds.

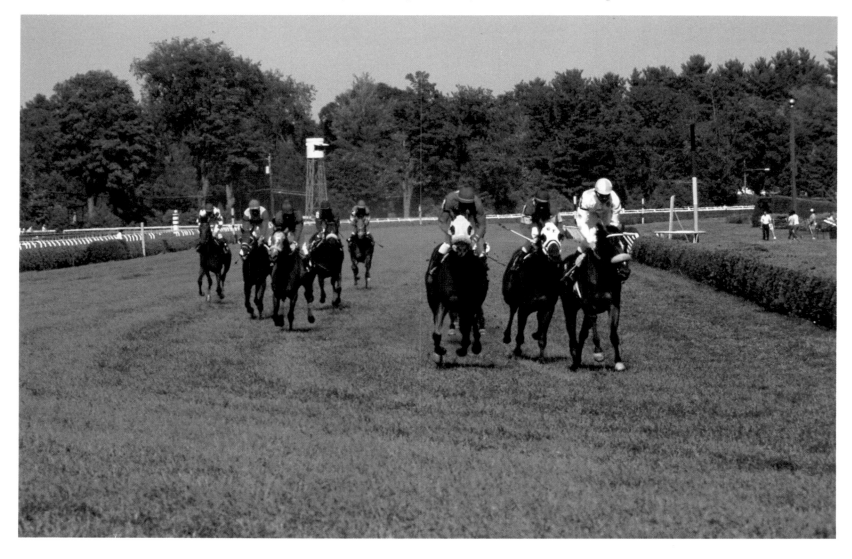

Winners of the Epsom Downs Derby

Year	Winner	Owner
1780	Diomed	Sir C Bunbury
1781	Young Eclipse	D O'Kelly
1782	Assassin	Lord Egremont
1783	Saltram	J Parker
1784	Serjeant	D O'Kelly
1785	Aimwell	Lord Clermont
1786	Nobel	T Panton
1787	Sir Peter Teazle	Lord Derby
1788	Sir Thomas	HRH Prince Of Wales
1789	Skyscraper	Duke of Bedford
1790	Rhadaman-thus	Lord Grosvenor
1791	Eager	Duke of Bedford
1792	John Bull	Lord Grosvenor
1793	Waxy	Sir F Poole
1794	Daedalus	Lord Grosvenor
1795	Spread Eagle	Sir F Standish
1796	Didelot	Sir F Standish
1797	(unnamed)	Duke of Bedford
1798	Sir Harry	J Cookson
1799	Archduke	Sir F Standish
1800	Champion	C Wilson
1801	Eleanor	Sir C Bunbury
1802	Tyrant	Duke of Grafton
1803	Ditto	Sir H Williamson
1804	Hannibal	Lord Egremont
1805	Cardinal Beaufort	Lord Egremont
1806	Paris	Lord Foley
1807	Election	Lord Egremont
1808	Pan	Sir H Williamson
1809	Pope	Duke of Grafton
1810	Whalebone	Duke of Grafton
1811	Phantom	Sir J Shelley
1812	Octavius	R Ladbroke
1813	Smolensko	Sir C Bunbury
1814	Blucher	Lord Stawell
1815	Whisker	Duke of Grafton
1816	Prince Leopold	HRH Duke of York
1817	Azor	J Payne
1818	Sam	T Thornhill
1819	Tiresias	Duke of Portland
1820	Sailor	T Thornhill
1821	Gustavus	J Hunter
1822	Moses	HRH Duke of York
1823	Emilius	J Udney
1824	Cedric	Sir J Shelley
1825	Middleton	Lord Jersey
1826	Lap-dog	Lord Egremont
1827	Mameluke	Lord Jersey
1828	Cadland	Duke of Rutland
1829	Frederick	GWK Gratwicke
1830	Priam	W Chifney
1831	Spaniel	Lord Lowther
1832	St Giles	R Ridsdale
1833	Dangerous	I Sadler
1834	Plenipo-tentiary	S Batson
1835	Mundig	J Bowes
1836	Bay Middleton	Lord Jersey
1837	Phosphorus	Lord Berners
1838	Amato	Sir G Heathcote
1839	Bloomsbury	W Ridsdale
1840	Little Wonder	D Robertson
1841	Coronation	AT Rawlinson
1842	Attila	G Anson
1843	Cotherstone	J Bowes
1844	Orlando	J Peel
1845	The Merry Monarch	GWK Gratwicke
1846	Pyrrhus the First	J Gully
1847	Cossack	TH Pedley
1848	Surplice	Lord Clifden
1849	The Flying Dutchman	Lord Eglinton
1850	Voltigeur	Lord Zetland
1851	Teddington	Sir J Hawley
1852	Daniel O'Rourke	J Bowes
1853	West Australian	J Bowes
1854	Andover	J Gully
1855	Wild Dayrell	FL Popham
1856	Ellington	OV Harcourt
1857	Blink Bonny	W l'Anson
1858	Beadsma	Sir J Hawley
1859	Musjid	Sir J Hawley
1860	Thormanby	J Merry
1861	Kettledrum	C Towneley
1862	Caractacus	C Snewing
1863	Macaroni	RC Naylor
1864	Blair Athol	W l'Anson
1865	Gladiateur	Comte F de Lagrange
1866	Lord Lyon	R Sutton
1867	Hermit	H Chaplin
1868	Blue Gown	Sir J Hawley
1869	Pretender	J Johnstone
1870	Kingcraft	Lord Ralmouth
1871	Favonius	Baron M de Rothschild
1872	Cremorne	H Savile
1873	Doncaster	J Merry
1874	George Frederick	WS Cartwright
1875	Galopin	Prince Batthyany
1876	Kisber	A Baltazzi
1877	Silvio	Lord Falmouth
1878	Sefton	WS Crawfurd
1879	Sir Bevys	Baron LN de Rothschild
1880	Bend Or	Duke of Westminster
1881	Iroquois	P Lorillard
1882	Shotover	Duke of Westminster
1883	St Blaise	Sir F Johnstone
1884	St Gatien (tie)	J Hammond
1884	Harvester (tie)	Sir J Willoughby
1885	Melton	Lord Hastings
1886	Ormonde	Duke of Westminster
1887	Merry Hampton	GA Baird
1888	Ayrshire	Duke of Portland
1889	Donovan	Duke of Portland
1890	Sainfoin	Sir J Miller
1891	Common	Sir F Johnston
1892	Sir Hugo	Lord Bradford
1893	Isinglass	H McCalmont
1894	Ladas	Lord Rosebery
1895	Sir Visto	Lord Rosebery
1896	Persimmon	HRH Prince of Wales
1897	Galtee More	J Gubbins
1898	Jeddah	JW Larnach
1899	Flying Fox	Duke of Westminster
1900	Diamond Jubilee	HRH Prince of Wales
1901	Volodyovski	WC Whitney
1902	Ard Patrick	J Gubbins
1903	Rock Sand	Sir J Miller
1904	St Armant	Leo de Rothschild
1905	Cicero	Leo de Rothschild
1906	Spearmint	E Loder
1907	Orby	R Croker
1908	Signorinetta	O Ginistrelli
1909	Minoru	HM the King
1910	Lemberg	AW Cox
1911	Sunstar	JB Joel
1912	Tagalie	W Raphael
1913	Aboyeur	AP Cunliffe
1914	Durbar	HB Duryea
1915	Pommern	SB Joel
1916	Fifinella	E Hulton
1917	Gay Crusader	AW Cox
1919	Gainsborough	Lady James Douglas
1919	Grand Parade	Lord Glanely
1920	Spion Kop	G Loder
1921	Humorist	JB Joel
1922	Captain Cuttle	Lord Woolavington
1923	Papyrus	B Irish
1924	Sansovino	Lord Derby
1925	Manna	HE Morriss
1926	Coronach	Lord Woolavington
1927	Call Boy	F Curzon
1928	Felstead	Sir H Cunliffe-Owen
1929	Trigo	W Barnett
1930	Blenheim	HH Aga Khan
1931	Cameronian	JA Dewar
1932	April the Fifth	T Walls
1933	Hyperion	Lord Derby
1934	Windsor Lad	HH Maharaja of Rajpipia
1935	Bahram	HH Aga Khan
1936	Mahmoud	HH Aga Khan
1937	Mid-day Sun	Mrs GB Miller
1938	Bois Roussel	P Beatty
1939	Blue Peter	Lord Rosebery
1940	Pont l'Evèque	F Darling
1941	Owen Tudor	Mrs R Macdonald-Buchanan
1942	Watling Street	Lord Derby
1943	Straight Deal	Miss D Paget
1944	Ocean Swell	Lord Rosebery
1945	Dante	Sir E Ohlson
1946	Airborne	JE Ferguson
1947	Pearl Diver	Baron G de Waldner
1948	My Love	HH Aga Khan
1949	Nimbus	Mrs M Glenister
1950	Galcador	M Boussac
1951	Arctic Prince	J McGrath
1952	Tulyar	HH Aga Khan
1953	Pinza	Sir V Sassoon
1954	Never Say Die	RS Clark
1955	Phil Drake	Mme L Volterra
1956	Lavandin	P Wertheimer
1957	Crepello	Sir V Sassoon
1958	Hard Ridden	Sir V Sassoon
1959	Parthia	Sir H de Trafford
1960	St Paddy	Sir V Sassoon
1961	Psidium	Mme A Plesch
1962	Larkspur	RR Guest
1963	Relko	F Dupre
1964	Santa Claus	J Ismay
1965	Sea-Bird	J Ternynck
1966	Charlottown	Lady Z Wernher
1967	Royal Palace	HJ Joel
1968	Sir Ivor	RR Guest
1969	Blakeney	AM Budgett
1970	Nijinsky	CW Engelhard
1971	Mill Reef	P Mellon
1972	Roberto	JW Galbreath
1973	Morston	AM Budgett
1974	Snow Knight	Mrs NF Phillips
1975	Grundy	C Vittadini
1976	Empery	NB Hunt
1977	The Minstrel	RE Sangster
1978	Shirley Heights	Lord Halifax
1979	Troy	Sir M Sobell
1980	Henbit	Mme A Plesch
1981	Shergar	HH Aga Khan
1982	Golden Fleece	RE Sangster
1983	Teenoso	EB Moller
1984	Secreto	L Miglietti
1985	Slip Anchor	Lord Howard de Walden
1986	Shahrastani	HH Aga Khan
1987	Reference Point	L Freedman
1988	Kahyasi	HH Aga Khan

Winners of the Kentucky Derby

Year	Horse	Owner	Year	Horse	Owner	Year	Horse	Owner	Year	Horse	Owner
1875	*Aristides*	HP McGrath	1908	*Stone Street*	CE & JW Hamilton	1936	*Bold Venture*	ML Schwartz	1966	*Kauai King*	Ford Stable
1876	*Vagrant*	William Astor	1909	*Wintergreen*	JB Respess	1937	*War Admiral*	Glen Riddle Farm	1967	*Proud Clarion*	Darby Dan Farm
1877	*Baden-Baden*	Daniel Swigert	1910	*Donau*	William Gerst	1938	*Lawrin*	Woolford Farm			
1878	*Day Star*	TJ Nichols	1911	*Meridan*	RF Carman	1939	*Johnstown*	Belair Stud	1968	*Forward Pass*	Calumet Farm
1879	*Lord Murphy*	George W Darden & Company	1912	*Worth*	HC Hallenbeck	1940	*Gallahadion*	Milky Way Farm	1969	*Majestic Prince*	Frank McMahon
1880	*Fonso*	JS Shawhan	1913	*Donerall*	TP Hayes	1941	*Whirlaway*	Calumet Farm			
1881	*Hindoo*	Dwyer Brothers	1914	*Old Rosebud*	HC Applegate	1942	*Shut Out*	Greentree Farm	1970	*Dust Commander*	Robert E Lehmann
1882	*Apollo*	Morris & Patton	1915	*Regret*	HP Whitney	1943	*Count Fleet*	Mrs John D Hertz			
1883	*Leonatus*	Chinn & Morgan	1916	*George Smith*	John Sanford	1944	*Pensive*	Calumet Farm	1971	*Canonero II*	Edgar Caibett
1884	*Buchanan*	William Cottrill	1917	*Omar Khayyam*	Billings & Johnson	1945	*Hoop Jr*	FW Hooper	1972	*Riva Ridge*	Meadow Stud, Inc
1885	*Joe Cotton*	JT Willimas				1946	*Assault*	King Ranch	1973	*Secretariat*	Estate of CT Chenery
1886	*Ben Ali*	JB Haggin	1918	*Exterminator*	WS Kilmer	1947	*Jet Pilot*	Maine Chance Farm			
1887	*Montrose*	Labold Brothers	1919	*Sir Barton*	JKL Ross				1974	*Cannonade*	JM Olin
1888	*MacBeth II*	Chicago Stable	1920	*Paul Jones*	Ral Parr	1948	*Citation*	Calumet Farm	1975	*Foolish Pleasure*	John L Greer
1889	*Spokane*	Noah Armstrong	1921	*Behave Yourself*	ER Bradley	1949	*Ponder*	Calumet Farm			
1890	*Riley*	Edward Corrigan				1950	*Middleground*	King Ranch	1976	*Bold Forbes*	ER Tizol
1891	*Kingman*	Jacobin Stable	1922	*Morvich*	Ben Block	1951	*Count Turf*	JJ Amiel	1977	*Seattle Slew*	Karen L Taylor
1892	*Azra*	Bashford Manor	1923	*Zev*	Rancocas Stable	1952	*Hill Gail*	Calumet Farm	1978	*Affirmed*	Harbor View Farm
1893	*Lookout*	Cushing & Orth	1924	*Black Gold*	Mrs RM Hoots	1953	*Dark Star*	Cain Hoy Stable	1979	*Spectacular Bid*	Hawksworth Farm
1894	*Chant*	Leigh & Rose	1925	*Flying Ebony*	GA Cochran	1954	*Determine*	AJ Crevolin			
1895	*Halma*	Byron McClelland	1926	*Bubbling Over*	Idle Hour Stock Farm	1955	*Swaps*	KC Ellsworth	1980	*Genuine Risk*	Mrs BR Firestone, Jr
1896	*Ben Brush*	MF Dwyer				1956	*Needles*	DH Stable			
1897	*Typhoon II*	JC Cahn	1927	*Whiskery*	HP Whitney	1957	*Iron Liege*	Calumet Farm	1981	*Pleasant Colony*	Buckland Farm
1898	*Plaudit*	JE Madden	1928	*Reigh Count*	Mrs JD Hertz	1958	*Tim Tam*	Calumet Farm			
1899	*Manuel*	AH & DH Morris	1929	*Clyde Van Dusen*	HP Gardner	1959	*Tomy Lee*	Mr & Mrs Fred Turner, Jr	1982	*Gato Del Sol*	Hancock & Peters
1900	*Lieutenant Gibson*	Charles H Smith	1930	*Gallant Fox*	Belair Stud				1983	*Sunny's Halo*	DJ Foster Stable
1901	*His Eminence*	FB VanMeter	1931	*Twenty Grand*	Greentree Stable	1960	*Venetian Way*	Sunny Blue Farm	1984	*Swale*	Claiborne Farm
1902	*Alan-a-Dale*	TC McDowell	1932	*Burgoo Kin*	ER Bradley	1961	*Carry Back*	Mrs Katherine Price	1985	*Spend A Buck*	Hunter Farm
1903	*Judge Himes*	Charles Ellison	1933	*Broker's Tip*	ER Bradley	1962	*Decidedly*	El Peco Ranch	1986	*Ferdinand*	Mrs Elizabeth Keck
1904	*Elwood*	Mrs CE Durnell	1934	*Cavalcade*	Brookmeade Stable	1963	*Chateaugay*	Darby Dan Farm	1987	*Alysheba*	Dorothy Pam Scharbauer
1905	*Agile*	SS Brown				1964	*Northern Dancer*	Windfields Farm			
1906	*Sir Huron*	George J Long	1935	*Omaha*	Belair Stud	1965	*Lucky Debonair*	Mrs Ada L Rice	1988	*Winning Colors*	Gene Klein
1907	*Pink Star*	J Hal Woodford									

Below: **The Kentucky Derby. Also included in the American Triple Crown: the Preakness at Pimlico, Maryland and the Belmont Stakes, at Belmont, New York.**

STEEPLECHASE JUMPING

The tradition of using horses for riding, cavalry, racing and hunting goes back for centuries. However, competition which involved jumping over structures made specifically for this purpose dates back less than a century. The sport was born when structures were first built on racetracks, with France leading the way in the sport's subsequent development. Dapper Henry Leclerc was their ace rider. He won many national and European championships, but was killed during the German invasion of his country in 1940.

Jumping events at today's meets consist of a rider guiding his horse through a set pattern of jumps over a timed course, with 'faults' given as penalties for mistakes. Faults may be incurred when the horse either refuses a jump or knocks down a bar during a jump.

Jumping has been an Olympic event since 1912, and today there are also world championship events, with points building toward international grand championship meets. Points are given in accordance with how a horse places at each of the individual meets, a system similar to that used in Grand Prix auto racing. By the turn of the century, high jumping was already an established, popular sport throughout the world. Records show that in 1906 Capitaine Georges Crousse, riding *Conspirateur*, an Australian Thoroughbred with a history of steeplechasing, cleared 7 feet, 8.8 inches at a meet in France. In 1912 Juge Montespieu cleared 7 feet, 9.2 inches. In 1933 Lt Christian de Castries of France, riding *Vol Au Vent*, jumped 7 feet, 10 inches. In 1938 Captain Antonio Gutierrez, an Italian riding *Ossopo*, cleared 8 feet, 0.4 inch.

In 1949 Captain Alberto Larraguibel broke the world's record on his third try by clearing 8 feet, 2.5 inches (2.47 meters). His horse, *Huaso*, was a 15-year-old Thoroughbred and former racehorse from Viña del Mar, Chile (near Santiago). He was a big horse, sired by *Henry Lee*. Another great Thoroughbred, *Chileno*, ridden by Lt Luis Riquelme, also competed that day. The record shows that when the bar was set at 2.14 meters, *Huaso* cleared it on his first try, *Chileno* on his second. At the height of 2.47 meters, *Chileno* did not even

Below: A steeplechase rider, with passenger. *At left:* Jump practice. *Below left:* Steeplechase competitors and friends. *At far left:* Silhouette of a jump.

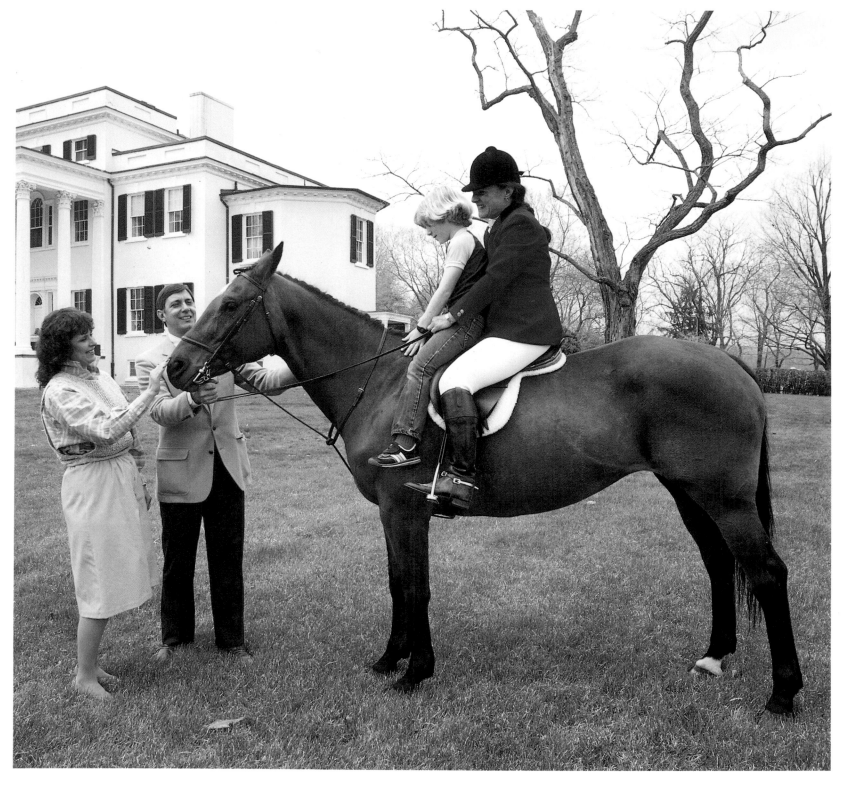

come close to clearing the bar on any of his attempts. *Huaso*, on his first attempt, knocked the top bar down, and on his second try he was out of step and refused. On his third try he cleared the bar cleanly. This writer has no knowledge of this record évery having been bettered *officially*.

The world broad jump record for horses was set in Spain in 1951 by *Amado Mio*, who was ridden by Col Fernando Lopez. The jump, 27 feet, 3.9 inches, still stood in 1975.

Because of his interest in horse sporting events, Baron de Coubertin, then president of the Olympic Committee, encouraged Count Clarence von Rosen, master of horse events to the king of Sweden, to make equestrian events part of the 1906 Olympic games. However, they were not included until 1912. At that time, ten nations sent 62 horses and 71 riders to compete. Russia entered with seven horses and riders, and the United States with four of each. (George M Patton was one of the team members.) Great Britain had four riders and five horses. The program included the 'Three Day Event,' also called the 'Military,' which was open only to officers on active duty. There was also a 'Steeplechase' event. Under the exceedingly stringent rules of the time, riders were eliminated quite quickly. Sweden made a clean sweep of medals in individual dressage, with their top competitor being Lt Nordlander. Captain Cariou on *Migson* and Count Bonde on *Emperior* also captured gold medals in this event.

Steeplechases, and the less strenuous 'Hunter Class' event, are now held all over the world. The 'Grand National Steeplechase,' held in Aintree, England, is probably the most widely known, as well as the most exciting and grueling, of these races. It consists of going twice around a two mile course, with two dozen difficult jumps, the most famous of which is

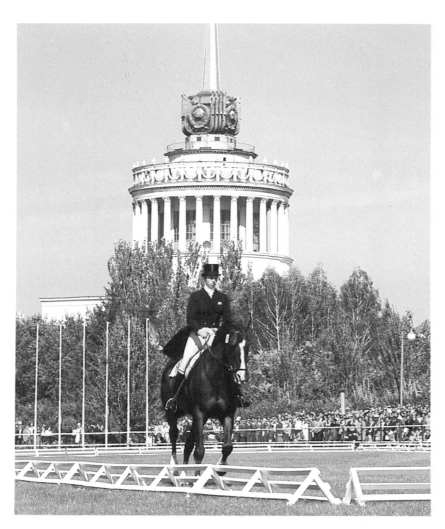

'Bechers Brook.' Both this steeplechase and the Bechers Brook jump were immortalized in the movie *National Velvet*, starring a teenage Elizabeth Taylor. The great horse *Red Run* won the Grand National twice and placed second once. In 1938 a small Thoroughbred horse, *Battleship*, which was sired by *Man o' War*, won this race against 31 other horses. He was 11 years old at the time. In another race which was televised, one of the front-runners, the only grey horse in the field, fell after a jump, throwing its rider. As both horse and rider struggled to their feet, the rest of the competitors streamed past them and over the jump! After mounting as quickly as possible, the unlucky rider was able to spur his horse on to a third place finish.

Prior to World War II steeplechasing, jumping, and the Nations Cup competitions were open only to military teams. When armies became fully mechanized, cavalry regiments were no longer needed, and so these sports were opened up to include civilian competitors. During the time when these competitions had been the exclusive domain of the military, public interest and support was minimal. Once the sports were expanded, public response was immediate and enthusiastic.

Many horses will not take to jumping, and if a horse does not naturally enjoy jumping there is little chance that it can ever be used in jumping sports. On the other hand, there are those that seem to have a natural aptitude for it and enjoy it as much as running. However, Thoroughbreds compose the majority of top jumping horses, with heights in the 17 hands range.

Below: A Thoroughbred in training tack. *Below opposite:* Competitors at a steeplechase in Lexington, Kentucky. *At far left:* A hedge jump — the competitor in the foreground has just made it. *At left:* Princess Anne of Great Britain at the European Equestrian Championships, 1973.

THE GRAND NATIONAL STEEPLECHASE
(The World's Greatest Race)

Steeplechase racing began near Aintree, England in the 1820s when a man named John Fromby ran some steeplechases, but his enterprise came to an end in 1835 when Lord Molyneux bought up the surrounding land and forced him out of business. Interest in the sport continued, and in 1837 the the first official Grand National steeplechase was run with four entrants. The winner was *The Duke*, owned by a Mr Sirdfield and ridden by a Mr Potts, whose weight was recorded as being 12 stone (168 lbs). The custom of listing the rider's weight in stone has continued to the present day.

In 1838 ten horses entered the race. *Sir William*, the favorite, was the winner. He was ridden by Captain Becher, who apparently was such an imposing figure that the most famous jump in the race was subsequently named after him. Other early jumps were dubbed Canal Turn, Valentines and Anchor Bridge. There were two dozen jumps in the four mile race (twice around a two mile track). As might be expected, from the beginning the race was dominated by English and Irish horses, with an occasional horse of Scottish ownership capturing top honors. Time records were not kept until 1863, when records show that the race lasted 11 minutes, 10 seconds.

In 1908 an American bred but English-trained 10-year-old named *Rubio* won in 10 minutes, 3 and ⅗ seconds. He was ridden by an Englishman named HB Bletsoe weighing 10 stone, five pounds. The following year a horse from France won for the first time. His name was *Parliament*, his time: nine minutes, 53 and ⅘ seconds. This record was tied in 1922 when *Music Hall* thundered home in first place. In 1933 another American owned, though English bred, horse called *Kellsboro Jack* came in first. He was owned by Mrs Ambrose Clark.

In 1938 *Battleship*, the first horse that was owned, bred, and also ridden by an American, was the winner. The smallest horse since *The Lamb* had covered the course in 1871, *Battleship* stood only 15.2 hands high. Sired by the famed *Man o' War*, he was owned by Mrs Marion Scott and ridden by 17-year-old Bruce Hobbs (11 stone, six pounds), the youngest jockey in the history of the race. Before the race was run, the little horse was all but overlooked, as the favorite, *Royal Danieli*, was so imposing in appearance and considered a sure bet to win. *Battleship* posted a time of nine minutes, 29 and ⅘ seconds, in his record-breaking run.

Other fast running times were turned in by *Teal* in 1952 (nine minutes, 20 and ⅗ seconds) and *Early Mist* in 1953 (nine minutes, 21 and ⅗ seconds).

Below: **Riders clear a hedge in the course of a steeplechase at Plains, Virginia.** *At right:* **A rider accustoms her horse to a jump.**

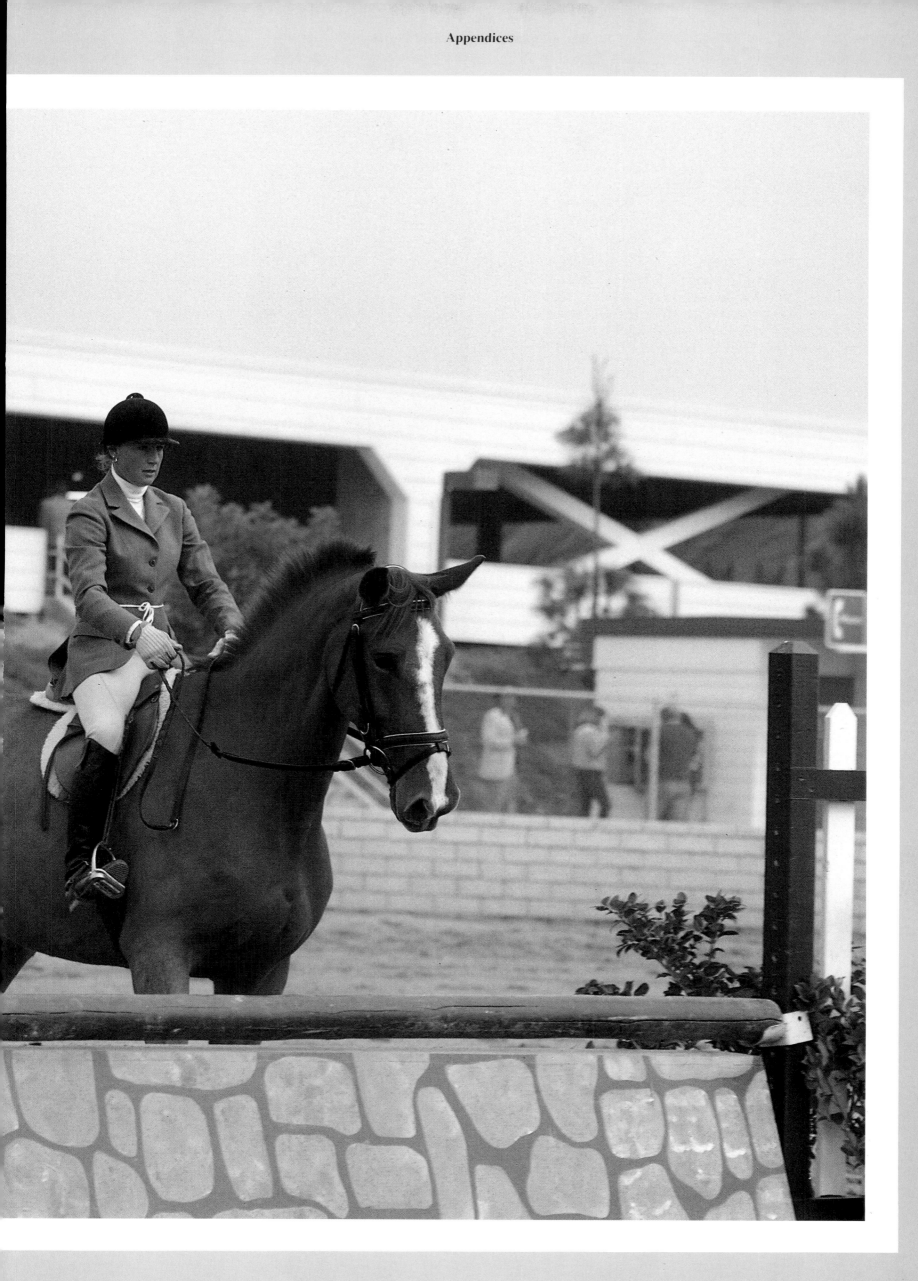

HARNESS RACING

As a general rule, the trotters and pacers used in harness racing are horses that are trotters and pacers by nature, although they are schooled to break the urge to fall into a gallop when they have reached high speed. It is generally accepted that pacers are slightly faster than trotters. Before they are allowed to race, they must be able to do the mile (1.6 km) in two minutes, 20 seconds, at their gait.

In the selective breeding of these horses, 'gait begets gait,' with each type of horse producing its own style of movement in their progeny. In the case of the pacer, both legs on one side of the animal move forward at the same time. The horse is usually equipped with a special harness, called a 'pacing hobble,' that discourages any tendency to break into a diagonal trot, or gallop. A famous pacer, *Dan Patch*, paced 20 different races, each in less than two minutes, from 1901 until his retirement in 1909. His record of 1:55.25, set in 1905, stood for 33 years.

The first harness horse — also a pacer — to race at less than two minutes was *Star Pointer*, who set a time of 1:59.25 on 28 August 1897. *Lou Dillon*, a trotter mare, made the mile in two minutes flat in Reidville, Massachusetts and in 1:55.5 in Memphis, Tennessee in 1903. Some other notable championship times are 1:55 by *Billy Direct* (1938), 1:55 by *Adios Harry* (1955) and 1:55.6 by *Adios Butler* (1960).

One of the greatest trotters of all time was *Greyhound*, sired by *Guy Abbey* out of *Elizabeth*. He was bred in the bluegrass country of Kentucky by Henry Hudson Knight, who also bred two other Hambletonian winners: *Yankee Maid* and *Chestertown*. At one time or another *Greyhound* held records at 14 different prestigious tracks. He trotted the mile in 1:55.5 on numerous occasions.

More recently *Bret Hanover* held the world record at 1:54, and in 1966 reduced his own time to 1:53.6.

Whenever harness racing is discussed, the American Standardbred comes immediately to mind. This breed was developed by crossing selected Thoroughbred stallions with selected grade mares. While in training, their front shoes are often weighted at the toe to induce a higher lift.

In 1788 a grey Thoroughbred stallion named *Messenger*, who had been winning races in England, was imported to the United States to stand at stud. His ancestry went back to the Darley Arabian through *Flying Childers*. His initial appearance in North America was not noteworthy, but the foals he sired were very fast, natural trotters.

The history of the Standardbred dates from *Messenger*. The mares chosen to mate with him were of the type that were adapted to driving. The purpose of this selective crossbreeding was to produce superior driving horses, with the accent on

Below: Harness racing at Saratoga. *At right:* Harness racing in Florida. *At far right:* Thoroughbred harness training. *Above right:* Riders and saddle horses on a western American trail in Arizona.

racing. By 1789, if a horse qualified by trotting a mile in 2:30 or by pacing the mile in 2:25, the horse was eligible for registration. This way, the 'standard' was established.

One of *Messenger*'s descendants, *Hambletonian*, a big, strong stallion out of a mare with Norfolk trotters in her ancestry, which also could be traced back to *Messenger*, was foaled in 1849. In the decades that followed, he and his progeny so dominated trotting races that other lines almost died out completely.

Today only horses of recorded Standardbred parentage are eligible for registration. The only other breeds that have any impact on the Standardbred are Morgans and Barbs. Standardbreds are not as large as Thoroughbreds, but their long forelegs and muscles enable them to extend to great speeds while trotting or pacing. They have influenced the nature of harness racing all over Europe, as well as in Russia, Australia and New Zealand.

Probably the most famous harness race held in the United States is the Hambletonian, run each summer at East Rutherford, New Jersey. In 1988 the trotter *Arbro Goal* won both heats of this $1,156,800 race. This three-year-old led practically every step of the way in both heats. His time for the first heat was 1:54.6, the fastest time ever recorded for a Hambletonian heat. His time for his second heat was 1:55.4, and again he set a new record by trotting the first half mile faster than any horse ever had in the 63 year history of the race. In the first heat, *Rule The Wind* placed second and *Firm Tribute* finished third. In the second heat, *Shaerpa Kosmas* was second and *Speedy Crown* came in third.

LONG DISTANCE RIDING

Long distance riding, or endurance racing, is probably the oldest of all equestrian sports. For centuries tales have been told of the great distances horses have carried their riders nonstop. In 1578, for instance, when the low countries were invaded by Spain, the pacifists were able to gain a momentary advantage over the Spaniards at Ghent, Belgium. According to Robert Browning's poem, 'How They Brought Good News From Ghent to Aix,' the citizenry of Ghent sent this good news via three Flemish horseback volunteers, one of whom was named Hassel Dirck. As the poem describes it, Hassel Dirck, urging his tired mount forward, cried, 'Stay spur, your Ruess has galloped bravely, the fault's not in her. We'll remember at Aix.' At that moment, 'his roan fell head and neck over, lay dead as a stone.'

In organized long distance rides there are checkpoints where large-animal veterinarians check each animal's heartbeat, respiration, temperature, and general overall condition, as well as the pasterns and feet, and look for signs of quivering muscles. Most races are between 50 to 100 miles in length, but a few are even longer. The smaller horses seem to be the most popular choice for mounts and yet, in the United States, the Arabian has the greatest number of wins and places. This may be due in part to the fact that a higher percentage of Arabians are entered.

Horse enthusiasts all have their own methods of conditioning their animals for this kind of competition. For instance, they will gallop their animals a given amount of time each day, with a proportion of both uphill and downhill running included. Some use the lunge line as part of the training each day. Those who have access to water practice swimming or galloping their horses in it. Some can afford special pools.

From time to time stories appear in horse magazines about unsupervised competitions where horses were literally ridden to death. In one instance, over a short period of time in one area, seven horses died in this manner. Thus, preparation for this kind of race is vital to the health and well-being of the animal. One must carefully consider the tack, the shoeing, the rider's clothing, and the feeding beforehand, and must study the leads of the animal during the training period. When the issue is life or death, each detail becomes an important factor.

BUCKING HORSES

Early rodeos, and the great riders who competed against one another in them, never would have come about had it not been for great bucking horses (aka *saddle broncs*). These horses are generally of mixed breed, with Quarter Horse and various draft horse blood (particularly that of the Percheron). Few Western horsemen have not heard of CB Irwin's *Steamboat*, who started bucking off the best rodeo riders in the state of Wyoming some 80 years ago. For the past 50 years, in fact, he has been commemorated in silhouette on the license plate of that state. It is said that he never failed to do his best to throw his riders, and he succeeded a majority of the time.

In years past, bucking horses were plentiful throughout the the large expanses of range country of northern Montana, Oregon, southern Alberta and Saskatchewan. Today rodeo stock contractors need to search hard to keep their bucking strings filled with satisfactory stock and, like everything else, the cost of really good horses has skyrocketed. In 1960, when Hoss Inman paid the EC Roberts Rodeo Company $2200 for the purebred Palomino bucking horse *Jesse James*, everyone considered it a whale of a price. The following year *Jesse James* was elected 'Bucking Horse of the Year' by the top 20 saddle bronc riders of the Professional Rodeo Cowboys Association. Not too many years later, the Big Bend Rodeo Company paid double the price for the great horse *Trails End*, when they purchased him from the heirs of Oral Zumwalt.

As an alternative, some people have tried to raise their own bucking horses. But because of the amount of range land required for even a single horse, and because once bought, there is still no guarantee that the animal will become a bucker and that the owner can recoup his investment through the horse's career, most attempts have been abandoned as too expensive. One group that *has* succeeded at raising its own bucking stock is the Calgary Stampede Association in Canada.

Spectators at rodeos often wonder about the breed of the bucking horses. Bucking horses in the saddle bronc event are, on the average, larger than the bareback event horses. Some saddle broncs will weigh 1600 pounds, so it is safe to assume that they have strong draft horse lineage in their breeding.

Around 1912 *Flying Devil*, a Montana saddle bronc, was known to have been ridden successfully only a very few times. He had a perfect Quarter Horse build, but the fact that the US Cavalry had Thoroughbred stallions quartered in the area points to the likelihood that he was also part Thoroughbred. Eastern Oregon's *Long Tom* had the marking and coloring of the Belgian and was large enough that there was assuredly some draft horse in him. The two great Canadian saddle broncs, *Midnight* and *Five Minutes to Midnight*, no doubt both had Percheron blood in them. Horses like *Big John*, another Canadian bronc, *War Paint* and *Wanda Dee* had to have had draft horse in their make-up. *Wanda Dee*, *Jesse James* and *Descent* were all Palominos. *Descent* and *Trails End* were known to have both Thoroughbred and Morgan blood. *Tipperary* looked like *Man o' War*'s twin. Those that have had success in raising bucking horses have bred bucking mares to bucking stallions, regardless of breed. As when breeding for racing, harness racing, jumping or dancing stock, the horse's ancestry dictates its performance.

In the 1930s there was another great bucking horse that grew up on the range lands of the Blackfeet Indian Reservation, not far from where *Descent* would later roam. This coal black horse, named simply *Blackfoot*, was used in rodeos all over northern Montana and southern Alberta, and was considered nearly unridable.

As the story is told, the Browning Rodeo had just ended and a group of professional riders had stopped for lunch before going on to the Calgary Stampede, which was scheduled to begin shortly. They fell to talking with some of the locals who told them that the area could boast many very skilled riders as well as excellent bucking horses. The locals claimed that their horses could buck off *anybody* who tried them.

The professional riders, who had held several world championships among themselves, decided they could pick up some easy money if they could get some bets, so they jollied the natives into raising as much bet money as they could.

The deal was made and bets were placed, and the black horse was led into the chute. One of the professionals, Hub Whiteman, who that year had made qualified rides on *Midnight*, *Five Minutes to Midnight* and *Hell's Angels* — three of the toughest horses on the rodeo circuit — was chosen to pick up the locals' money by riding their black horse. Due to his large size, he was not a man to win a lot of rides, but he was known for his skill at successfully riding the tougher horses. The black horse was tough, but not tough enough.

Another tale is told about the great liver chestnut colored champion, *Trails End*. Joe Kelsey of the Big Bend Rodeo Company bought him from the Zumwalt Rodeo heirs. At that time, the Big Bend Rodeo Company also owned a very good bay bucking horse that had twice been voted the top bucking horse in saddle bronc competitions at the National Finals Rodeo. His name was *Trade Winds*.

From the moment the two great bucking horses got together, they became the best of buddies. This is not an uncommon thing with horses; they, too, have best friends, not unlike children on a playground.

During the last weekend of July 1969 the Big Bend Rodeo stock was being used at the Vinson Ranch PRCA Rodeo at Thompson Falls, Montana. In the saddle bronc event *Trails End* had bucked his rider off but was still loose in the arena when the chute boss opened the chute gate and let *Trade Winds* and his rider out. *Trade Winds* proceeded to buck his rider off, leaving the two horses loose in the arena with their empty saddles on. They started nickering and whinnying to each other, and quickly got together in the center of the arena, touching noses like a mare and foal. When the back gate was opened they ran side-by-side out of the arena. After they were unsaddled and set loose in the stock pen, they remained at each other's side.

In 1956 the rodeo contractors and the Professional Rodeo Cowboys Association decided to name a champion saddle bronc as 'Bucking Horse of the Year' (BHOY). They are drawn from the best such horses from throughout North America. At the end of the year the 20 top money winners among the saddle bronc riders would vote on the horses that had been nominated by their owners. A big black and white Pinto horse named *War Paint*, raised on the Klamath Indian Reservation in Oregon and owned by the Christensen brothers, won the silver halter that year and the next. He richly deserved the award; for the four previous years he had bucked off nearly every rider who drew him. Any rider who was lucky enough to make a qualified ride on *War Paint* knew that he was definitely on his way to the pay window.

Joker, owned by Harry Knight of Fowler, Colorado, was the winner the third year. In 1958 the riders had voted a tie between him and *War Paint*. In 1959 *Trails End* of the Zumwalt Rodeo Company captured the title. That year the National Finals Rodeo was held for the first time, and *Trails End*'s performance at the Dallas, Texas Finals earned him the top title there, as well. The next year he was again elected National Finals Champion.

The first ten years of the National Finals found *Trails End* on its roster nine times. *Trails End* was followed to the top spot by *Jake*, *Jesse James* and *Big John* (who made it twice), then *Wanda Dee* of the Calgary Stampede string, followed again by *Jake*.

In the spring of 1961, on the ranch of Arthur R 'Doug' Douglas, 20 miles north of Browning and seven miles southeast of Babb, Montana, a colt was foaled. Its sire was a grandson of *Plenipotentiary*, a Thoroughbred stallion that the Glacier National Park horse concessioner and the Bar X6 Ranch had

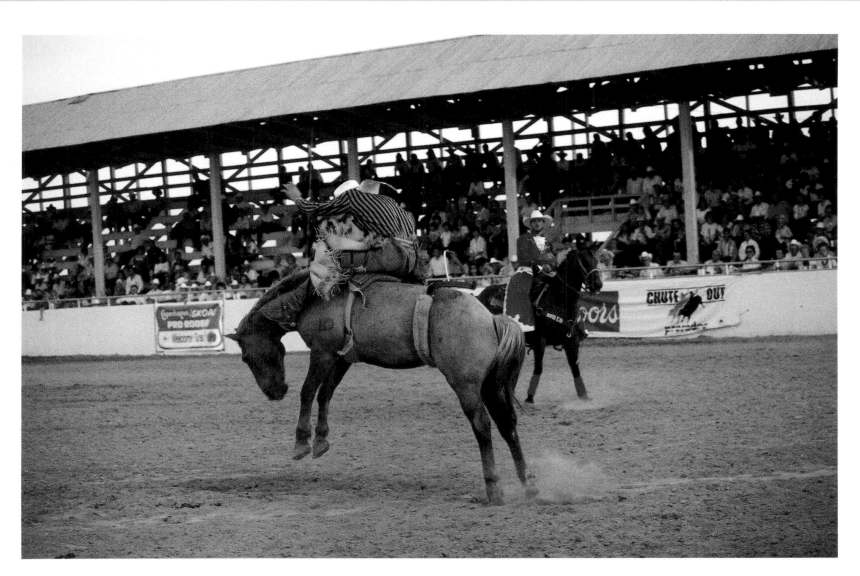

Above and below: **A Quarter Horse and its rider, in a classic 'bronc riding' exhibition at the West of the Pecos Rodeo in Pecos, Texas.**

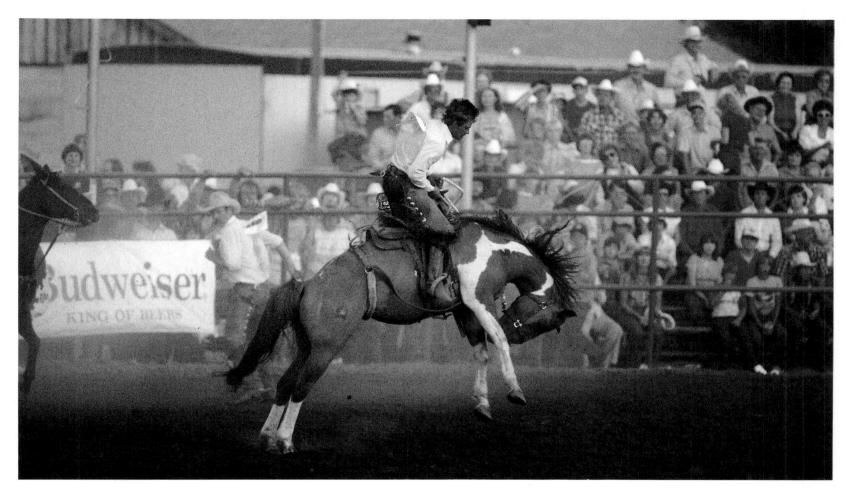

Above: Having stayed atop this Pinto for the allotted time period, a 'saddle bronc' rider grabs the reins with both hands. *Below:* Bareback bronc riding.

used on loan from the US Army Remount Station. *Pleni-potentiary* was a half brother of *Man o' War*, both having been sired by *Fairplay*. The colt's mother was a very fine grade mare who was part Morgan.

In 1964, when the colt was three, he was still 'rough' — only partly broken to ride. In his fourth year, he was let out to range with a band of half-wild horses in the Chief Mountain area on the east slope of the Continental Divide in the Northern Rockies. In winter, the band would come down to the flatlands on the Blackfeet Indian reservation which surrounded the Douglas ranch.

In the spring of 1965, when the colt was five, he was at last corralled and saddled. He bucked the first man to try him. Subsequently, one experienced rider after another tried him but none could manage to stay on. Douglas hired the horse out to Hugo Johnson, an outfitter living in St Mary, Montana, just outside Glacier National Park, who used him as a pack horse in the nearby Bob Marshall Wilderness. Hugo, though a seasoned hand, was unable to gentle the horse, so he returned him to Douglas. Douglas then sold him to a horse dealer named Eddie Vaughn, who in turn sold him to a rodeo stock contracting company named Beutler Brothers and Cervi. They gave the big five-year-old dappled Palomino gelding the name *Descent*.

By the end of *Descent*'s first half season on the rodeo circuit, no rider had been able to complete a qualified ride. That year Harry Knight's bronc *Jake* won the Bucking Horse of the Year award. In *Descent*'s second year, 1966, the only man to successfully ride him was the 1963 world champion bronc rider, Guy Weeks. Among his other victims were Shawn Davis, the 1965 champion, and Alvin Nelson, the 1967 champion. He was voted Bucking Horse of the Year champion in 1966, as well as the following three years. In 1970, *Descent* was injured in a trucking accident and did not rejoin the circuit until the

Below: The saddle bronc shown here obviously has draft horse blood in his lineage. *Overleaf:* This equestrienne's steed evidences some Quarter Horse blood. *Page 192:* A Pinto saddle horse. Horse and rider — a timeless image.

following year, when he completely recovered. When he came back, he again captured the top honor for two seasons running (1971 and 1972). His six BHOY titles compiled a record that will probably stand for many years.

In 1988, at the age of 18, he was still going strong. While waiting in the chute before a ride, *Descent* still holds his head up, nostrils flaring, in anticipation of what he's going to do to the next cowboy for the following eight seconds.

Following is a list of Bucking Horses of the Year awards furnished by the Professional Rodeo Cowboys Association in Colorado Springs, Colorado. Each one of these broncs, in order to earn this honor, have done so by tossing 95% of the riders that have drawn them. The list reflects the best broncs in North America.

BUCKING HORSE OF THE YEAR AWARDS 1956–1988

Horse	Year	Owner	Horse	Year	Owner
War Paint	1956	Christensen Brothers	Sam Bass	1973	Jiggs Beutler
War Paint	1957	Christensen Brothers	Checkmate	1974	Bob Christensen
Joker	1958 (tie)	Harry Knight	Frontier Airlines	1975	Beutler Brothers & Cervi
War Paint	1958 (tie)	Christensen Brothers	Sarcee Sorrel	1976	Harry & Wayne Vold
Trails End	1959	Oral Zumwalt Rodeo Company	Crystal Springs	1977	Bob Barnes
Jake	1960	Harry Knight	Angel Sings	1978	Harry Vold
Jesse James	1961	Hoss Inman	Deep Water	1979 (tie)	Jim Sutton
Big John	1962	Harry Knight	Angel Sings	1979 (tie)	Harry Vold
Big John	1963	Harry Knight	Brookman's Velvet	1980	Cervi Championship
Wanda Dee	1964	Calgary Stampede Association	Rusty	1981	Harry Vold Rodeo Company
Jake	1965	Harry Knight	Buckskin Velvet	1982	Flying U Rodeo Company
Descent	1966	Beutler Brothers & Cervi	Alibi	1983	Del Hall
Descent	1967	Beutler Brothers & Cervi	Try Me	1984	Wayne Vold
Descent	1968	Beutler Brothers & Cervi	Blow Out	1985	Beutler & Son
Descent	1969	Beutler Brothers & Cervi	Wrangler Savvy	1986	Harry Vold Rodeo Company
Rodeo News	1970	Reg Kesler	Challenger & Skoal	1987	Beutler & Son
Descent	1971	Beutler Brothers & Cervi	Skoal's Alley Cat	1988	Greg Kesler
Descent	1972	Beutler Brothers & Cervi			

BAREBACK BUCKING HORSE OF THE YEAR AWARDS 1956–1988

In 1974, the Professional Rodeo Cowboys Association and the Rodeo Contractors started giving Bucking Horse of the Year awards to bareback broncs, as they had to saddle broncs since 1956. This list is furnished by the Professional Rodeo Cowboys Association in Colorado Springs, Colorado.

Horse	Year	Owner	Horse	Year	Owner
Moonshine	1974	Reg Kesler	Classic Velvet	1981	Flying U Rodeo Company
Stormy Weather	1975	Steiner	Smith & Velvet	1982	Bobby Christensen
Moon Rocket	1976	Calgary Stampede Association	Sippin' Velvet	1983	Bernis Johnson
Mr Smith	1977	Christensen Brothers	Sippin' Velvet	1984	Bernis Johnson
Sippin' Velvet	1978	Bernis Johnson	Tombstone	1985	Jim Sutton
Smith & Velvet, née Mr Smith	1979	Christensen Brothers	Sippin' Velvet	1986	Bernis Johnson
Smith & Velvet	1980	Christensen Brothers	Skoal's Sippin' Velvet	1987	Bernis Johnson
			Kingsway Skoal	1988	Vern Franklin